The Second Amendment:
A History of the Right to Keep and Bear Arms in America

"A well regulated Militia, being necessary to the security of a free State, the right of the people to keep and bear Arms, shall not be infringed."

The Second Amendment to the United States Constitution

THE SECOND AMENDMENT

A HISTORY OF THE RIGHT TO KEEP AND BEAR ARMS IN AMERICA

TIMOTHY LUDWIG

RARE BOOK
PUBLISHING LLC
RareBookPublishing.com

The Second Amendment:
A History of the Right to Keep and Bear Arms in America
From Colonial Roots to Modern Freedom

Copyright © 2025 Timothy Ludwig

All rights reserved. No part of this publication may be reproduced, distributed, or transmitted in any form or by any means, including photocopying, recording, or other electronic or mechanical methods, without the prior written permission of the publisher, except in the case of brief quotations embodied in critical reviews and certain other noncommercial uses permitted by copyright law.

First Edition

ISBN: 979-8-9998265-1-0 (paperback)

Library of Congress Control Number: 2025921764

Published by Rare Book Publishing LLC
rarebookpublishing.com

For information about special discounts for bulk purchases, please contact the publisher.

Book design, editorial and creative direction by Timothy Ludwig

The author has made every effort to ensure the accuracy of the information contained in this book. However, the information is provided "as is" without warranty of any kind. The author and publisher disclaim any liability for any damages resulting from the use of this information.

This book contains documented historical accounts, legal analysis, and constitutional interpretation related to the Second Amendment and firearms in American history. While every effort has been made to verify the accuracy of historical facts and legal precedents, readers should consult qualified legal professionals for current legal advice regarding firearms laws and regulations.

The views expressed in this book are those of the author and do not necessarily reflect the official policy or position of any government agency, organization, or institution.

Printed in the United States and on demand through various international printing facilities.

Table of Contents

Introduction: The Shot Heard 'Round the World 1

Part 1: Colonial Foundations (1600-1783)
Chapter 1: Breaking the Chains of Tyranny 7
Chapter 2: The American Frontier - A Test of Survival 9
Chapter 3: The Road to Revolution 15
Chapter 4: 1776 - The Declaration of Independence 21

Part 2: Forging a New Nation (1783-1860)
Chapter 5: The Wisdom of the Founding Fathers 29
Chapter 6: The Birth of the Second Amendment 37
Chapter 7: 1791 - The Year Freedom Was Secured 47

Part 3: A Nation Divided and Rebuilt (1860-1900)
Chapter 8: The Civil War Era - Industry vs. Ingenuity 55
Chapter 9: The Fight for Universal Freedom 63
Chapter 10: The Wild West - Where Legends Were Born 69

Part 4: The Modern Era (1900-Present)
Chapter 11: American Innovation and the Spirit of Enterprise 85
Chapter 12: The Supreme Court Restores the Second Amendment 91
Chapter 13: The Strength of American Gun Culture 93
Chapter 14: America Armed and Free - The Numbers Tell the Story 97
Chapter 15: The American Way - Guns as Part of Our Heritage 101
Chapter 16: The Future of Freedom 105
Conclusion: The Eternal Flame of Freedom 109
Appendix A: Key Constitutional Texts 111
Appendix B: Key Historical Documents 112
Appendix C: Firearms of the Civil War 113
Timeline of the Second Amendment 115
Sources 117
Index 119-121
About The Author 123

Introduction:
The Shot Heard 'Round the World

The story of the Second Amendment begins not in a stuffy room with powdered-wigged men, but on a village green, with the smell of gunpowder in the air. It begins with a single shot, a shot that would echo through the centuries and become a symbol of American liberty. The shot heard 'round the world.

On April 19, 1775, a small band of colonial militiamen gathered on the Lexington town green, facing a much larger force of British soldiers. The British had come to seize the colonists' weapons, to disarm them and crush their growing rebellion. But the colonists would not be disarmed. They stood their ground, and when the smoke cleared, the American Revolution had begun.

This book is the story of the right that those men fought and died for: the right to keep and bear arms. It is a story that is deeply intertwined with the story of America itself, a story of freedom, self-reliance, and the enduring struggle to preserve our constitutional rights.

We will travel back in time to the forests of colonial America, where the flintlock musket was a tool of survival and a symbol of independence. We will sit in on the debates of the Constitutional Convention, where the Founding Fathers wrestled with the question of how to create a government that was strong enough to protect the people, but not so strong that it would threaten their liberties.

We will ride with the cowboys of the Wild West, who have been both celebrated and vilified for their use of firearms. We will meet the heroes and villains of the gun culture wars, from the sharpshooters of the 19th century to the activists of the 21st.

And through it all, we will explore the meaning and purpose of the Second Amendment, a right that has been the subject of intense debate and controversy, but which remains a cornerstone of American freedom.

This is not a book that will tell you what to think about guns. It is a book that will give you the facts, the history, and the stories you need to make up your own mind. It is a book that will take you on a journey through the heart of

American history, a journey that will leave you with a deeper understanding of the Second Amendment and its enduring importance in our lives.

So let us begin our journey, not with a political debate, but with a story. A story of a brave woman who used a firearm to defend herself and her family from a violent attacker. A story that reminds us that the right to keep and bear arms is not an abstract legal concept, but a real and tangible means of preserving life and liberty.

A Mother's Courage: The Story of Sarah McKinley

On New Year's Eve 2011, eighteen-year-old Sarah McKinley was alone in her rural Oklahoma home with her three-month-old baby when she heard someone trying to break in. Her husband had died of cancer just days earlier on Christmas Day, leaving her a young widow with an infant to protect.

Sarah called 911, but she knew help was minutes away and the danger was immediate. Two men were outside her home - one was trying to break down her door while the other served as a lookout. She could hear them talking about what they planned to do once they got inside.

"I've got two guns in my hand," Sarah told the 911 dispatcher. "Is it okay to shoot him if he comes in the door?"

The dispatcher told her she had the right to defend herself and her baby. Sarah positioned herself in her bedroom, placed her infant son in his crib, and waited with a 12-gauge shotgun and a pistol. When 24-year-old Justin Martin finally broke through her door and entered her home with a large hunting knife, Sarah didn't hesitate. She fired one shot, stopping the threat immediately.

The second intruder fled the scene and was later arrested. Police investigation revealed that Martin had a history of drug-related crimes and had specifically targeted Sarah's home because he believed a young widow would be an easy victim.

Sarah McKinley became a symbol of courage and the importance of the Second Amendment. Her story spread across the nation, reminding millions of Americans why the right to keep and bear arms matters. Without that right, Sarah and her baby might not have survived that terrifying night.

"I wouldn't have done it, but it was my baby," Sarah said later. "It was my baby, and I had to protect him."

This is why the Second Amendment exists. Not for abstract political debates, but for real moments when real people face real threats. Sarah McKinley's story is the story of the Second Amendment - the story of ordinary Americans who refuse to be victims, who take responsibility for their own safety and the safety of their loved ones.

Her courage that New Year's Eve connects her to a long line of Americans who have understood that freedom isn't free, and that sometimes the price of liberty is the willingness to defend it. From the colonial militiamen who faced British soldiers on Lexington Green to the pioneers who carved civilization out of the wilderness, Americans have always understood that the right to keep and bear arms is the right that preserves all other rights.

Now let us travel back in time to discover how this fundamental right came to be, and how it has shaped the American story from the very beginning.

Part 1:
The Colonial Foundations
(1600-1783)

Chapter 1:
Breaking the Chains of Tyranny

The right to keep and bear arms, enshrined in the Second Amendment of the United States Constitution, is not a uniquely American concept. Its roots run deep into the soil of English history, drawing sustenance from centuries of legal precedent, political philosophy, and the lived experience of the English people. To understand the American right, we must first understand its English inheritance.

The Glorious Revolution of 1688 stands as a pivotal moment in this story. The overthrow of King James II, a Catholic monarch who sought to disarm his Protestant subjects, led to the enactment of the English Bill of Rights in 1689. This landmark document, a cornerstone of English constitutional law, declared, "That the subjects which are Protestants may have arms for their defence suitable to their conditions and as allowed by law."[1]

This was not an unlimited right. It was restricted to Protestants and was subject to legal regulation. But it was a right nonetheless, a right that was born out of the fear of tyranny and the belief that an armed citizenry was a necessary check on the power of the state. This idea, that the people have a right to defend themselves against a tyrannical government, would become a central tenet of American revolutionary thought.

The colonists also inherited a deep-seated distrust of standing armies. In England, professional armies were seen as a tool of the monarchy, a threat to the liberty of the people. The preferred alternative was the militia, a citizen army that could be called upon in times of crisis, but which would then return to civilian life. This preference for the militia over the standing army was reflected in the political philosophy of the Whigs, who had a profound influence on the American colonists.

Early colonial gun laws reflected this dual heritage. On the one hand, there was a strong emphasis on the importance of an armed citizenry. Laws were passed requiring men to own firearms and to participate in militia musters. On the other hand, there were also regulations on the use and storage of firearms, as well as restrictions on who could own them. The goal was to strike a balance between the right to bear arms and the need for public safety.

This, then, was the English inheritance of the American colonists: a right to bear arms that was rooted in the fear of tyranny, a deep-seated distrust of standing armies, and a belief in the importance of a well-regulated militia. It was a complex and sometimes contradictory inheritance, but it would provide the foundation for the Second Amendment and the American tradition of gun ownership.

[1] "English Bill of Rights 1689," The Avalon Project, Yale Law School, accessed September 8, 2025, https://avalon.law.yale.edu/17th_century/england.asp.

Chapter 2:
The American Frontier - A Test of Survival

The vast and untamed wilderness of the American frontier played a crucial role in shaping the colonial mindset and solidifying the importance of firearms for survival and self-defense. Life on the frontier was a constant struggle against the elements, a struggle that demanded self-reliance, resourcefulness, and the ability to defend oneself and one's family from a variety of threats.

Conflicts with Native American tribes were a brutal reality of frontier life. While some interactions were peaceful, many were marked by violence and bloodshed. The colonists, outnumbered and isolated, relied on their firearms to defend their settlements and to project power into the interior. The gun was a tool of both offense and defense, a symbol of the colonists' determination to claim the land as their own.

King Philip's War, which raged in New England from 1675 to 1678, was one of the deadliest of these conflicts. The war, which pitted the English colonists against a confederation of Native American tribes led by the Wampanoag chief Metacomet, also known as King Philip, was a brutal and bloody affair. It was a war of raids and ambushes, a war in which the flintlock musket was the primary weapon of both sides. The colonists, who were ultimately victorious, learned a valuable lesson from the war: the importance of a well-armed and well-organized militia.

But the gun was not just a weapon of war on the frontier. It was also an essential tool of everyday life. The colonists hunted for food, for furs, and for trade. They used their firearms to protect their livestock from predators and to defend their homes from intruders. The gun was a constant companion, a symbol of the colonists' mastery over the wilderness and their ability to provide for themselves and their families.

This, then, was the legacy of the American frontier: a deep-seated belief in the importance of firearms for survival and self-defense, a belief that was forged in the crucible of conflict and hardship. It was a belief that would be carried into the revolutionary era and would find its ultimate expression in the Second Amendment.

The Story of Hannah Duston: Courage and Self-Defense on the Colonial Frontier

Perhaps no story better illustrates the harsh realities of colonial frontier life and the fundamental principles that would later inspire the Second Amendment than that of Hannah Duston, a remarkable woman whose courage and determination made her the first American woman to be honored with a public monument.

Hannah Emerson Duston was born in 1657 and lived in Haverhill, Massachusetts, during one of the most dangerous periods in colonial history. King William's War was raging, and raids by French-allied Native American warriors were a constant threat to English colonial settlements. These were not abstract political conflicts fought by distant armies - they were life-and-death struggles that came right to people's doorsteps.

On March 15, 1697, Hannah's world changed forever. She was a 40-year-old mother of eight children, recovering from childbirth just one week earlier with her newborn daughter Martha. Her husband Thomas was working in the fields when a war party of Abenaki warriors attacked Haverhill. The raiders struck swiftly and without warning, burning homes and taking captives.

Hannah was at home with baby Martha and her neighbor Mary Neff, who was helping care for the infant. When the attack began, Thomas raced back toward his house but realized he could not reach his wife and baby in time. Faced with an impossible choice, he gathered his other children and fled to safety, hoping against hope that Hannah and the baby would somehow survive.

The Abenaki warriors captured Hannah, baby Martha, and Mary Neff, along with several other colonists. They began the long march north toward Canada, where captives were typically either ransomed back to their families or adopted into Native American communities. For Hannah, still weak from childbirth and carrying her infant daughter, the journey was a nightmare.

Tragically, baby Martha did not survive the first day of the march. The infant died, leaving Hannah devastated and filled with a mother's grief and rage. For two weeks, the captives were forced to march through the wilderness, sleeping on the ground and eating whatever food their captors provided.

Eventually, the main war party split up, and Hannah and Mary were left with a smaller group consisting of two Abenaki men, three women, and seven children, along with another English captive - a 14-year-old boy named Samuel Leonardson who had been captured from Worcester, Massachusetts, a year and a half earlier. Samuel had learned the Abenaki language and customs during his captivity.

Hannah, however, was not content to accept her fate as a captive. She was a colonial woman who understood that survival often depended on decisive action and the willingness to fight for one's life and freedom. She began to formulate a plan for escape - a plan that would demonstrate the same principles of self-defense that would later be enshrined in the Second Amendment.

Recognizing that Samuel's knowledge of Abenaki customs could be crucial, Hannah convinced him to ask one of the warriors to teach him the proper way to kill someone with a tomahawk. The warrior, perhaps thinking this was merely a boy's curiosity about warfare, obligingly demonstrated the technique, showing Samuel exactly where and how to strike for a quick, silent kill.

On the night of April 30, 1697, Hannah put her plan into action. The Abenaki family was sleeping peacefully, trusting their captives enough not to post guards or restrain them. In the early hours before dawn, Hannah, Mary, and Samuel armed themselves with tomahawks and moved silently among the sleeping figures.

What happened next was swift and decisive. The three captives killed ten of their captors - the two men, three women, and five children. Only an elderly woman and one small boy managed to escape in the darkness. Hannah and her companions then scalped their victims, following the grim frontier custom of the time, which would serve as proof of their deed and entitle them to bounty payments from the colonial government.

Taking a canoe, the three survivors began their journey down the Merrimack River toward Massachusetts. They traveled for several days, navigating by the stars and avoiding detection, until they finally reached safety in the colonial settlements. When they arrived in Boston, they presented the ten scalps to the Massachusetts General Assembly and received a reward of fifty pounds - a substantial sum at the time.

Hannah Duston's story spread quickly throughout the colonies and became one of the most famous captivity narratives of the colonial period. The influential Puritan minister Cotton Mather wrote about her ordeal multiple times, portraying her as a righteous woman who had struck back against those who had murdered her child and threatened her life.

But Hannah's story is about more than just survival or even revenge. It is fundamentally a story about the principles that would later be enshrined in the Second Amendment. Hannah Duston found herself in a situation where no government, no army, and no law enforcement could help her. She was on her own, hundreds of miles from civilization, with only her own courage and determination to rely upon.

Her story illustrates several crucial principles that would later guide the Founding Fathers. First, it demonstrates that the right to defend oneself is a natural right that exists regardless of what any government says. Hannah did not ask permission to defend herself - she simply did what was necessary to survive and regain her freedom.

Second, it shows that effective self-defense sometimes requires the use of weapons and the willingness to use them decisively. Hannah and her companions could not have escaped through negotiation or passive resistance. They needed weapons, they needed the knowledge of how to use them effectively, and they needed the moral courage to act when the moment came.

Third, Hannah's story demonstrates that ordinary citizens - including women - can and must be prepared to defend themselves when circumstances require it. Hannah was not a soldier or a professional fighter. She was a mother and a homemaker. But when her life and freedom were at stake, she proved capable of extraordinary courage and effectiveness.

The colonial authorities' decision to reward Hannah and her companions with fifty pounds was significant. It represented official recognition that their actions were not only justified but praiseworthy. The colonial government understood that frontier survival depended on citizens who were willing and able to defend themselves.

Hannah Duston's story became legendary throughout colonial America and remained popular well into the 19th century. She was eventually honored with not one but three public monuments - making her the first American woman to be memorialized in this way. These monuments recognized her not as a killer, but as a defender of freedom and a symbol of American courage and self-reliance.

Her story also illustrates the broader context in which the Second Amendment was later written. The Founding Fathers lived in a world where Hannah Duston's experience was not unique. They understood that government could not always protect its citizens, that evil existed in the world, and that good people sometimes had to fight for their lives and freedom.

When they wrote that "the right of the people to keep and bear Arms, shall not be infringed," they were thinking of people like Hannah Duston - ordinary Americans who might find themselves in extraordinary circumstances, with no one to rely on but themselves. They understood that the right to keep and bear arms was not about hunting or sport, but about the fundamental human right to defend one's life, family, and freedom.

Hannah Duston lived to be 79 years old, dying in 1736. She remarried after her ordeal and continued to live on the Massachusetts frontier. Her story reminds us that American freedom was not won easily or without cost. It was secured by ordinary people who were willing to fight for it when necessary, and who understood that freedom requires both vigilance and the means to defend it.

The lesson of Hannah Duston's story is not that violence is good, but that sometimes good people must be prepared to use force to defend themselves against those who would do them harm. It is a lesson that the Founding Fathers understood well, and it is one of the reasons why they enshrined the right to keep and bear arms in the Constitution. In a dangerous world, the ability to defend oneself is not just a right - it is a necessity.

"In the darkest hour, courage is not the absence of fear —
it is the will to rise and defend what must not be lost."

Chapter 3:
The Road to Revolution

The revolutionary period was a time of profound transformation in the American colonies. It was a time when the colonists, who had once been loyal subjects of the British Crown, rose up in rebellion and declared their independence. And it was a time when the right to bear arms, which had long been a practical necessity, became a political right, a right that was essential for resisting tyranny.

The Stamp Act of 1765, which imposed a tax on all printed materials in the colonies, was a major turning point in the road to revolution. The colonists, who had no representation in the British Parliament, saw the tax as a violation of their rights as Englishmen. They organized protests and boycotts, and they formed armed groups like the Sons of Liberty to resist the enforcement of the tax. The militia, which had once been a tool of the colonial governments, became a symbol of colonial defiance.

The Boston Massacre of 1770, in which British soldiers fired on a crowd of colonists, killing five, further inflamed revolutionary sentiment. The incident was used as propaganda by patriots like Paul Revere, who created a famous engraving of the massacre that depicted the British soldiers as brutal aggressors and the colonists as innocent victims. The massacre reinforced the colonists' fear of standing armies and their belief that an armed citizenry was necessary to protect them from government overreach.

The Battles of Lexington and Concord on April 19, 1775, were the spark that ignited the Revolutionary War. The British, who were determined to disarm the colonists, marched on Concord to seize a cache of arms and ammunition. But the colonists, who had been warned of the British advance, were ready for them. The minutemen, a special unit of the colonial militia, confronted the British at Lexington and Concord, and the "shot heard 'round the world" was fired.

The Revolutionary War was a long and bloody struggle, but it was a struggle that the colonists ultimately won. And they won it, in large part, because they were an armed people. They were a people who believed in the right to keep and bear arms, and they were a people who were willing to fight and die for that right. This, then, was the legacy of the revolutionary era: a deep and abiding belief that the right to bear arms was not just a right, but a sacred duty, a duty to defend oneself, one's family, and one's country from the threat of tyranny.

Daniel Boone and the Defense of Boonesborough: Courage on the Kentucky Frontier

Among the most heroic episodes of the Revolutionary War was the defense of Boonesborough, Kentucky, in September 1778. This dramatic siege showcased the courage, ingenuity, and marksmanship skills that would become legendary in American frontier history. At the center of this epic defense was Daniel Boone, the famous frontiersman whose name became synonymous with American courage and the pioneering spirit.

Daniel Boone was born in Pennsylvania in 1734, but he made his mark in the wilderness of Kentucky, which was then considered the edge of the known world. Boone was not just an explorer and hunter - he was a visionary who saw the potential for American settlement in the rich lands beyond the Appalachian Mountains. In 1775, he established Boonesborough as one of the first permanent settlements in Kentucky, creating a foothold for American civilization in the wilderness.

The settlement of Boonesborough was more than just a collection of cabins - it was a symbol of American determination and the westward expansion that would define the nation's character. The fort was built in a rectangle, with blockhouses at each corner and a stockade connecting them. Inside the walls were cabins, a meeting house, and storage areas for supplies and ammunition. The design was both practical and defensive, reflecting the dangerous realities of frontier life.

By 1778, the Revolutionary War had reached the Kentucky frontier. The British, seeking to prevent American expansion westward, had formed alliances with several Native American tribes, including the Shawnee, who saw the American settlements as a threat to their traditional hunting grounds. The stage was set for a confrontation that would test the courage and resolve of the American pioneers.

The crisis began in February 1778 when Daniel Boone was captured while making salt at Blue Licks, about forty miles from Boonesborough. Boone and twenty-seven other men had been taken prisoner by a large Shawnee war party led by Chief Blackfish. The Shawnee planned to use Boone's knowledge of Boonesborough's defenses to capture the fort and drive the Americans out of Kentucky.

But Daniel Boone was not an ordinary prisoner. He was a master of frontier diplomacy and psychological warfare. Rather than trying to escape immediately, Boone convinced Chief Blackfish to adopt him as a son, gaining the chief's trust and learning valuable intelligence about Shawnee plans. For four months, Boone lived among the Shawnee, all the while gathering information about their military capabilities and intentions.

In June 1778, Boone learned that the Shawnee were planning a massive attack on Boonesborough in September, when they expected to have 400 warriors and British support. Realizing that the fort was in mortal danger, Boone made his escape, traveling 160 miles through the wilderness in just four days to warn the settlement.

When Boone arrived at Boonesborough on June 20, 1778, he found the fort in a state of near-abandonment. Many families had fled to safer areas, and only about 50 people remained, including women and children. The fort's defenses were in poor condition, and ammunition was running low. It seemed impossible that such a small force could withstand an attack by 400 warriors.

But Daniel Boone was not a man to give up easily. He immediately began preparing the fort for siege, organizing the defenders and strengthening the fortifications. He knew that the key to survival would be accurate rifle fire from the fort's walls, and he made sure that every man and boy who could shoot was armed and ready.

Boone also understood the importance of morale. He knew that the defenders would need to believe they could win if they were going to fight effectively. He shared his knowledge of Shawnee tactics and weaknesses, and he emphasized that their superior marksmanship and defensive position gave them significant advantages over their attackers.

The siege began on September 7, 1778, when Chief Blackfish arrived with a force of about 400 Shawnee warriors and a few British officers. The attackers greatly outnumbered the defenders, but Boone had prepared well. The fort's walls were strong, the defenders were well-positioned, and every man was armed with a reliable rifle.

Blackfish initially tried to negotiate, demanding that the fort surrender. He even offered to allow the defenders to leave peacefully if they would abandon Boonesborough. But Boone and the other leaders refused. They knew that surrendering would mean the end of American settlement in Kentucky, and they were determined to fight for their homes and their future.

The siege that followed was a masterpiece of defensive warfare. The Shawnee warriors tried every tactic they knew - direct assault, fire arrows, tunneling under the walls, and psychological warfare. But the defenders, led by Boone's tactical genius and inspired by his courage, repelled every attack.

The key to the defense was the exceptional marksmanship of the Kentucky riflemen. These men had grown up hunting in the wilderness, and they could place a rifle ball exactly where they wanted it at ranges that amazed even experienced warriors. The Shawnee, who were accustomed to fighting enemies armed with smoothbore muskets, found themselves facing opponents who could hit individual targets at distances of 200 yards or more.

One of the most dramatic moments of the siege occurred when the Shawnee attempted to tunnel under the fort's walls. Boone discovered the tunnel and organized a counter-mining operation, digging their own tunnel to intercept the attackers. When the tunnels met, a fierce underground battle ensued, with both sides fighting in the darkness with knives and tomahawks. The Americans eventually prevailed, collapsing the Shawnee tunnel and ending that threat.

Throughout the siege, the defenders maintained their discipline and morale despite being vastly outnumbered. They rationed their ammunition carefully, making every shot count. They took turns on watch duty, ensuring that the walls were always manned. And they supported each other through the long days and nights of constant danger.

The women and children of Boonesborough also played crucial roles in the defense. They loaded rifles, carried ammunition, tended the wounded, and maintained the fires that provided light for the defenders. Some of the women were skilled shots themselves and took positions on the walls alongside the men.

After eleven days of siege, the Shawnee finally withdrew. They had suffered significant casualties while inflicting minimal losses on the defenders. The siege had failed, and with it, the British plan to drive the Americans out of Kentucky. Boonesborough had held, and American expansion westward would continue.

The defense of Boonesborough was significant for several reasons. First, it demonstrated the importance of firearms in protecting American settlements on the frontier. Without their rifles, the defenders could never have held off such a large attacking force. The superior accuracy and range of the American rifles gave them a decisive advantage over their enemies.

Second, the siege showed the importance of leadership and tactical skill. Daniel Boone's knowledge of Native American warfare, his ability to inspire his men, and his tactical innovations were crucial to the successful defense. He proved that American frontiersmen could not only survive in the wilderness but could also defend their communities against overwhelming odds.

Third, the defense of Boonesborough illustrated the broader principles that would later be enshrined in the Second Amendment. The settlers were defending not just their lives but their right to live freely in the land they had chosen. They were exercising the fundamental right of free people to defend themselves, their families, and their communities against those who would drive them out or destroy them.

The technical aspects of the defense were remarkable. The Kentucky long rifle, which was the primary weapon of the defenders, was one of the most accurate firearms of its time. These rifles were handcrafted by skilled gunsmiths, often German immigrants who had brought their expertise to America. The rifles had spiral grooves cut into the barrel (rifling) that spun the bullet and greatly improved accuracy.

The Kentucky riflemen were also masters of marksmanship. They practiced constantly, competing with each other in shooting contests and hunting expeditions. They understood the ballistics of their weapons, the effects of wind and weather on their shots, and the importance of careful aim and steady nerves under pressure.

The siege of Boonesborough also demonstrated the importance of community cooperation and mutual support. The defenders were not professional soldiers but ordinary settlers - farmers, hunters, and craftsmen who had come to Kentucky seeking a better life. But when their community was threatened, they came together and fought as one, each person contributing their skills and courage to the common defense.

Daniel Boone's leadership during the siege made him a legend throughout America. His story was told and retold, inspiring countless other Americans to push westward and claim new lands for the growing nation. He became a symbol of American courage, ingenuity, and determination - qualities that would define the American character for generations to come.

The successful defense of Boonesborough also had important strategic consequences. It secured Kentucky for American settlement and opened the way for further westward expansion. The victory demonstrated that American settlers could defend themselves against any enemy, no matter how numerous or determined.

After the siege, Boonesborough continued to grow and prosper. More settlers arrived, attracted by the rich land and the security provided by the fort's successful defense. The settlement became a model for other frontier communities, showing how Americans could establish civilization in the wilderness while maintaining their ability to defend themselves.

The legacy of Boonesborough extends far beyond the events of September 1778. The siege became a symbol of American determination and the importance of the right to keep and bear arms. It showed that free people, properly armed and led, could defend themselves against any threat. It demonstrated that the Second Amendment was not just about individual rights but about the collective ability of American communities to protect themselves and preserve their way of life.

Today, the story of Daniel Boone and the defense of Boonesborough reminds us of the courage and sacrifice of the men and women who built America. It shows us that freedom is not free, and that sometimes good people must be willing to fight to preserve it. And it illustrates the timeless truth that the right to keep and bear arms is essential for protecting all the other rights that make life worth living.

Chapter 4:
1776 - The Declaration of Independence and the Right of Revolution

The year 1776 stands as the most important year in the history of human freedom. It was the year when a group of brave American colonists did something that had never been done before in human history - they declared that governments exist only by the consent of the governed, and that when a government becomes destructive of the people's rights, it is not only the right but the duty of the people to alter or abolish it.

The Declaration of Independence, adopted on July 4, 1776, was more than just a statement of political separation from Great Britain. It was a revolutionary manifesto that established the philosophical foundation for all future American thinking about government, liberty, and the right to keep and bear arms.

"We hold these truths to be self-evident," wrote Thomas Jefferson in those immortal words, "that all men are created equal, that they are endowed by their Creator with certain unalienable Rights, that among these are Life, Liberty and the pursuit of Happiness." This was revolutionary thinking - the idea that rights come not from government, but from God, and that governments are created to protect those rights, not to grant them.

But perhaps even more revolutionary was what came next: "That whenever any Form of Government becomes destructive of these ends, it is the Right of the People to alter or to abolish it, and to institute new Government, laying its foundation on such principles and organizing its powers in such form, as to them shall seem most likely to effect their Safety and Happiness."

This was the philosophical foundation for what would later become the Second Amendment. The Declaration established the principle that the people have not just the right, but the duty, to resist tyrannical government. And how can an unarmed people resist a tyrannical government? They cannot. The right to revolution necessarily implies the right to keep and bear arms.

The Declaration went on to list the specific grievances against King George III, many of which involved the use of military force against the colonists. The King had "kept among us, in times of peace, Standing Armies without the Consent of our legislatures." He had made the military "independent of and superior to the Civil power." He had imposed taxes without consent and "deprived us in many cases, of the benefits of Trial by Jury."

These grievances would later be addressed in the Constitution and Bill of Rights. The Third Amendment would prohibit the quartering of soldiers in private homes. The Sixth Amendment would guarantee trial by jury. And the Second Amendment would ensure that the people would always have the means to resist tyranny.

The Declaration also recognized that the colonists had tried peaceful means of redress: "In every stage of these Oppressions We have Petitioned for Redress in the most humble terms: Our repeated Petitions have been answered only by repeated injury." When peaceful means fail, the Declaration implied, other means become necessary.

The signing of the Declaration was an act of incredible courage. The fifty-six men who signed it knew they were committing treason against the British Crown, and that if they failed, they would likely hang. Benjamin Franklin captured the moment perfectly when he said, "We must, indeed, all hang together or, most assuredly, we shall all hang separately."

But they also knew they were creating something unprecedented in human history - a nation founded on the principle that government exists to serve the people, not the other way around. They were creating a nation where the people would retain the ultimate power, including the power to defend themselves against tyranny.

The Declaration of Independence established the intellectual framework that would guide American thinking about government and individual rights for centuries to come. It established the principle that rights are natural and God-given, not government-granted. It established the principle that governments derive their just powers from the consent of the governed. And it established the principle that the people have the right and duty to resist tyrannical government.

These principles would later be enshrined in the Constitution and Bill of

Rights, including the Second Amendment. The right to keep and bear arms is not just about hunting or sport shooting - it is about the fundamental right of free people to defend themselves against tyranny, a right that was first proclaimed to the world in the Declaration of Independence on that glorious Fourth of July in 1776.

Nancy Hart: The War Woman of Georgia

The spirit of 1776 was not limited to the men who signed the Declaration of Independence or fought in the Continental Army. Throughout the colonies, ordinary Americans - including remarkable women like Nancy Hart - took up arms to defend their homes, their families, and their newfound freedom. Nancy's story is one of the most extraordinary tales of courage and marksmanship from the Revolutionary War, proving that the spirit of liberty burned just as brightly in the hearts of American women as it did in the hearts of American men.

Nancy Morgan Hart was born around 1735 in North Carolina, but she made her mark in the Georgia backcountry, where she and her husband Benjamin carved out a homestead in the wilderness along the Broad River. Nancy was a formidable woman in every sense - tall, strong, and possessed of a fierce independence that would serve her well in the dangerous years of the Revolution. She was also an excellent shot with both rifle and pistol, skills that would prove crucial when the war came to her doorstep.

The Georgia frontier during the Revolution was a particularly brutal theater of conflict. Unlike the more formal battles fought in the North, the war in Georgia was characterized by vicious partisan fighting between Patriots and Loyalists, with both sides often targeting civilians. British forces and their Loyalist allies regularly raided Patriot settlements, burning homes, stealing livestock, and terrorizing families. It was in this environment that Nancy Hart would earn her legendary reputation.

Nancy's first recorded act of defiance occurred early in the war when a group of Loyalist raiders came to her cabin demanding information about Patriot activities in the area. Nancy, who was known for her quick wit as well as her marksmanship, pretended to be a simple frontier woman with no knowledge of military matters. She invited the men to sit down for a meal, all the while gathering intelligence about their plans and numbers.

As the Loyalists relaxed and began to drink, Nancy excused herself to tend to her cooking. What they didn't realize was that she was actually loading her husband's rifle, which she kept hidden near the fireplace. When she returned to the room, she had the weapon concealed beneath her apron. At the right moment, she drew the rifle and held the entire group at gunpoint, forcing them to surrender their weapons.

But Nancy's most famous exploit occurred later in the war when a group of six British soldiers arrived at her cabin. These men were not on a military mission - they were deserters who had been living off the land by robbing and terrorizing isolated homesteads. They had heard that Nancy's husband was away, and they thought they could easily intimidate a lone woman into providing them with food and shelter.

They could not have been more wrong. Nancy welcomed the soldiers into her home with apparent hospitality, offering to cook them a meal. The men, pleased with their apparent good fortune, stacked their muskets in the corner and settled down to wait for their dinner. What they didn't know was that Nancy was planning something far different from a simple meal.

As Nancy worked at the fireplace, she began to carefully move the soldiers' muskets, one by one, through a gap in the cabin's log walls to her daughter, who was waiting outside. The process required incredible nerve and skill - one wrong move, one suspicious glance from the soldiers, and Nancy would have been discovered and likely killed.

When Nancy had successfully moved three of the six muskets outside, one of the soldiers noticed what was happening. He jumped up and shouted a warning to his companions, but Nancy was ready for him. She grabbed one of the remaining muskets and leveled it at the group, ordering them to surrender.

The soldiers, realizing they had been outmaneuvered by a frontier woman, tried to rush her. Nancy's response was swift and deadly - she shot the first man through the heart, killing him instantly. Before the others could reach her, she had grabbed a second musket and wounded another soldier. The remaining men, faced with a woman who was clearly a better shot than any of them, threw up their hands in surrender.

Nancy held the surviving soldiers at gunpoint until her neighbors arrived to help secure the prisoners. The wounded soldier died of his injuries, and the three survivors were turned over to Patriot authorities. Nancy's cabin became famous throughout the Georgia backcountry as the place where one woman had single-handedly defeated a squad of enemy soldiers.

But Nancy Hart's contributions to the Patriot cause went far beyond this single dramatic incident. She served as a spy and scout for the Continental forces, using her knowledge of the local terrain and her ability to move undetected through the wilderness to gather intelligence on British and Loyalist activities. Her information helped Patriot forces plan successful raids and avoid enemy ambushes.

Nancy also served as a messenger, carrying vital communications between Patriot commanders across the dangerous Georgia frontier. This was incredibly hazardous work - messengers who were captured by the enemy faced torture and execution. But Nancy's skill with firearms and her intimate knowledge of the backcountry allowed her to complete these missions successfully time and again.

The technical aspects of Nancy's marksmanship were remarkable for her time. She was skilled with both rifles and smoothbore muskets, and she understood the importance of maintaining her weapons in perfect condition. In an era when most firearms were single-shot weapons that required careful loading and priming, Nancy's ability to quickly and accurately engage multiple targets was extraordinary.

Nancy's story also illustrates the important role that women played in the Revolutionary War, particularly on the frontier. While they may not have served in formal military units, women like Nancy Hart were essential to the Patriot war effort. They defended their homes, gathered intelligence, carried messages, and provided support to the Continental forces. Their courage and sacrifice were every bit as important as the contributions of the men who fought in the formal battles of the war.

After the war, Nancy Hart became a legendary figure in Georgia. The state honored her memory by naming a county after her, and her story was passed down through generations of Georgians as an example of the courage and determination that had won American independence. She became known as the "War Woman," a title that reflected both her martial prowess and her fierce dedication to the cause of liberty.

Nancy's story also demonstrates the importance of the principles that would later be enshrined in the Second Amendment. Her ability to defend herself and her family with firearms was not just a matter of personal protection - it was a crucial element in the broader struggle for American independence. Without women like Nancy Hart, who were willing and able to take up arms in defense of freedom, the Revolution might well have failed.

The legacy of Nancy Hart extends far beyond her individual exploits. She represents the spirit of American independence - the idea that free people have not only the right but the duty to defend themselves against tyranny. Her story reminds us that the Second Amendment is not just about the right to own firearms, but about the broader principle that a free people must always be prepared to defend their liberty.

Nancy Hart died in 1830, having lived to see the young nation she had helped to create grow and prosper. But her legacy lives on in the countless American women who have followed her example, taking up arms to defend their families, their communities, and their country. She proved that courage, skill, and determination are not limited by gender, and that the spirit of liberty burns just as brightly in the hearts of American women as it does in the hearts of American men.

Today, as we face new challenges and new threats to our freedom, the example of Nancy Hart remains as relevant as ever. She reminds us that liberty is not a gift that can be taken for granted, but a precious inheritance that must be defended by each generation. She shows us that ordinary Americans, armed with courage and the means to defend themselves, can overcome any enemy and preserve the blessings of freedom for future generations.

"Liberty's flame burns not in the strength of men alone, but in the fierce resolve of every soul who dares to defend it."

Part 2:
Forging a New Nation
(1783-1860)

Chapter 5:
The Wisdom of the Founding Fathers

The Constitutional Convention of 1787 stands as one of the greatest gatherings of political genius in human history. In the sweltering heat of a Philadelphia summer, fifty-five of America's brightest minds came together to create something the world had never seen before: a government designed to protect individual liberty while maintaining the strength necessary to defend the nation. Their wisdom in crafting this delicate balance would prove to be one of humanity's greatest achievements in the science of government.

The victory in the Revolutionary War had given the American people their independence, but it had also presented them with an extraordinary opportunity - the chance to build a government from scratch, based on the lessons learned from centuries of human experience with power and tyranny. The Founding Fathers understood that they were not just creating a government for their own time, but establishing principles that would guide future generations in the preservation of liberty.

The Intellectual Giants Behind the Second Amendment

The men who gathered in Philadelphia during that historic summer brought with them not just political experience, but a deep understanding of history, philosophy, and human nature that would prove essential in crafting the Second Amendment. Their collective wisdom drew from centuries of study, personal experience with tyranny, and an unwavering commitment to human liberty.

George Washington, the presiding officer of the Convention, brought unique credibility to discussions of military affairs and citizen soldiers. As commander of the Continental Army, Washington had witnessed firsthand the courage and effectiveness of citizen-soldiers who had taken up arms to defend their liberty. He understood that America's victory had come not from professional soldiers alone, but from farmers, merchants, and craftsmen who had left their plows and workshops to fight for freedom.

"A free people ought not only to be armed, but disciplined," Washington would later write, capturing the essence of what would become the Second Amendment. His vision was of a nation where every citizen was both capable of and responsible for defending liberty. This was not the vision of a military dictator, but of a leader who understood that true security came from an armed and trained citizenry.

The debates over military power at the Constitutional Convention revealed the profound wisdom of these remarkable men. They had just fought a war against a tyrannical government that had used a standing army to oppress the people, and they were determined never to allow such tyranny to take root in America. Yet they also understood that the new nation would need the ability to defend itself against foreign enemies and domestic threats.

James Madison: The Scholar-Statesman's Revolutionary Vision

James Madison, the "Father of the Constitution," brought to Philadelphia a mind steeped in the study of government and history. Madison had spent months preparing for the Convention by studying every form of government known to history, from ancient Greece and Rome to the modern republics of his day. His notes and research filled volumes, and his conclusions would shape not just the Constitution but the entire American experiment in self-government.

Madison understood that the right to bear arms was not just about military defense - it was about the fundamental relationship between government and the governed. In his famous Federalist 46, Madison would later explain that an armed American citizenry represented a force of "nearly half a million of citizens with arms in their hands, organized under governments possessing their affections and confidence."

This was Madison's revolutionary insight: that in America, unlike in Europe, the people themselves would be the ultimate military force. European armies numbered in the tens of thousands; American citizen-soldiers could number in the hundreds of thousands. This arithmetic of liberty meant that no American government could ever become tyrannical without facing overwhelming resistance from its own people.

Madison's vision went beyond mere numbers. He understood that an armed citizenry represented a different kind of political relationship - one where the government served at the pleasure of the people, not the other way around. This was the intellectual foundation of the Second Amendment: the recognition that political liberty and the right to bear arms were inseparable.

Alexander Hamilton: The Practical Visionary

Alexander Hamilton brought to the Constitutional Convention a unique combination of military experience and financial genius. As Washington's aide-de-camp during the Revolution, Hamilton had seen how citizen-soldiers could defeat professional armies when fighting for their homes and families. As America's first Secretary of the Treasury, he would later understand how an armed citizenry contributed to economic prosperity by providing security for commerce and property.

The solution they crafted was nothing short of brilliant. They created a system where the federal government would have the power to raise armies when necessary, but where the ultimate military power would remain in the hands of the people themselves through the militia system. This was revolutionary thinking - a government that derived its power from the people and that trusted the people to remain armed and ready to defend their liberty.

Hamilton's contributions to the Federalist Papers revealed his deep understanding of the relationship between arms and liberty. In Federalist 28, he argued that when government overreached, "the citizens must rush tumultuously to arms, without concert, without system, without resource; except in their courage and despair."

But Hamilton's vision was more sophisticated than simple resistance to tyranny. He understood that an armed citizenry would actually make government more stable and effective by ensuring that it remained responsive to the people's needs. A government that knew its citizens were armed would be more careful to govern justly and effectively.

The Federalists, led by visionaries like Hamilton and Madison, understood that America needed a strong central government to survive in a dangerous world. But they also understood that this strength must never come at the expense of individual liberty. The Anti-Federalists, champions of individual rights like Patrick Henry and George Mason, insisted that any new government must include explicit protections for the rights of the people.

George Mason: The Architect of Rights

George Mason of Virginia brought to the constitutional debates a lifetime of experience in crafting protections for individual rights. As the author of the

Virginia Declaration of Rights, Mason had already articulated many of the principles that would later appear in the Bill of Rights, including the right to bear arms.

Mason's Virginia Declaration stated that "a well-regulated militia, composed of the body of the people, trained to arms, is the proper, natural, and safe defense of a free state." This language would directly influence the Second Amendment, but Mason's contribution went deeper than mere words.

Mason understood that rights were not created by government but were inherent in human nature. His vision was of a constitution that would recognize and protect these natural rights, not grant them as privileges. This philosophical foundation was essential to the Second Amendment's ultimate meaning and purpose.

The genius of the Constitutional Convention was that it brought these two perspectives together and forged them into a single, coherent vision of government. The result was a Constitution that created a federal government with enough power to function effectively, while preserving the rights of the states and the people to maintain their own defense forces.

Mason's insistence that the Constitution include a Bill of Rights reflected his understanding that written protections were necessary to prevent future governments from infringing on the people's natural rights. His walkout from the Constitutional Convention when his proposed Bill of Rights was rejected demonstrated his unwavering commitment to individual liberty.

Patrick Henry: The Voice of the People

Patrick Henry, though not present at the Constitutional Convention, represented the voice of millions of Americans who insisted that any new government must include explicit protections for individual rights. Henry's opposition to the Constitution without a Bill of Rights forced the Federalists to confront the fundamental question: could the people trust their government to respect their rights without explicit constitutional protections?

Henry's famous declaration, "Give me liberty, or give me death!" captured the spirit that would animate the Second Amendment. For Henry and millions of Americans like him, liberty was not a gift from government but a natural right that government existed to protect. The right to bear arms was simply the practical means of ensuring that this protection would be effective.

Henry's concerns about standing armies reflected the experience of a generation that had lived under British military occupation. "A well-regulated militia, composed of the freeholders, citizen and husbandman, who take up arms to preserve their property as individuals, and their rights as freemen," Henry argued, was the only military force compatible with liberty.

Article I, Section 8 of the Constitution reflects this wisdom perfectly. It gives Congress the power to "provide for calling forth the Militia to execute the Laws of the Union, suppress Insurrections and repel Invasions" and to "provide for organizing, arming, and disciplining, the Militia." But it also reserves to the states "the Appointment of the Officers, and the Authority of training the Militia according to the discipline prescribed by Congress."

This was more than just a political compromise - it was a stroke of genius that recognized a fundamental truth about human nature and government. The Founding Fathers understood that power corrupts, and that the only way to prevent tyranny was to ensure that the ultimate power remained in the hands of the people themselves.

The Practical Wisdom of Roger Sherman

Roger Sherman of Connecticut brought to the Constitutional Convention the practical wisdom of a man who had risen from humble beginnings to become one of America's most respected leaders. As the only person to sign all four of America's founding documents (the Continental Association, the Declaration of Independence, the Articles of Confederation, and the Constitution), Sherman understood better than anyone the evolution of American thinking about government and liberty.

Sherman's contribution to the Second Amendment debates was his practical understanding of how militias actually worked. As a former militia officer, Sherman knew that effective citizen-soldiers required not just the right to bear arms but also the training and organization necessary to use those arms effectively.

Sherman's vision of the militia was not of a ragtag collection of armed citizens, but of a well-organized force capable of defending the community against any threat. This vision required not just individual gun ownership but also community organization, training, and leadership - all of which would be protected by the Second Amendment.

The International Perspective: Lafayette's Influence

The Marquis de Lafayette, though not an American, played a crucial role in shaping American thinking about the right to bear arms. As a young French volunteer who had fought alongside Washington in the Revolution, Lafayette understood how American citizen-soldiers differed from European professional armies.

Lafayette's letters to European friends described the American militia system as a revolutionary innovation that made tyranny impossible. "In America," Lafayette wrote, "every citizen is a soldier, and every soldier is a citizen. This makes the people unconquerable and the government accountable."

The debates at the Constitutional Convention laid the intellectual foundation for what would become the Second Amendment. The Founding Fathers understood that an armed citizenry was not just a military necessity, but a political necessity - the final check on government power and the ultimate guarantee of individual liberty.

The Economic Foundation of Freedom

The Founding Fathers understood that the right to bear arms was not just about political liberty but also about economic prosperity. In an age when government could not provide police protection to every community, an armed citizenry was essential for protecting commerce, property, and economic development.

Benjamin Franklin, though elderly during the Constitutional Convention, brought a lifetime of experience as a businessman and diplomat. Franklin understood that America's economic future depended on the security that only an armed citizenry could provide. His famous observation that "those who would give up essential liberty to purchase a little temporary safety deserve neither liberty nor safety" reflected his understanding that true security came from an armed and vigilant people, not from government protection.

Hamilton's economic vision for America also depended on the Second Amendment. He understood that commerce and industry required security, and that in a vast nation like America, this security could only be provided by an armed citizenry capable of protecting their communities, their property, and their economic activities.

The Religious Dimension of Natural Rights

Many of the Founding Fathers understood the right to bear arms in religious terms, seeing it as part of God's plan for human liberty and dignity. This religious understanding of the right to bear arms provided a moral foundation that went beyond mere political theory.

The Reverend Dr. John Witherspoon, president of Princeton College and the only clergyman to sign the Declaration of Independence, taught that the right of self-defense was a God-given right that no government could legitimately infringe. Witherspoon's influence on Madison and other Founding Fathers helped establish the theological foundation for the Second Amendment.

This religious understanding of the right to bear arms was not limited to any single denomination. Protestant, Catholic, and Jewish leaders all recognized that the ability to defend oneself and one's family was a fundamental aspect of human dignity that reflected the image of God in man.

These remarkable men had studied history, and they knew that every free society that had disarmed its citizens had eventually fallen to tyranny. They were determined that America would be different, that it would be a nation where the people retained the means to defend their freedom against all enemies, foreign and domestic.

The Enduring Legacy of Constitutional Wisdom

The Constitutional Convention was more than just a political gathering - it was a meeting of minds dedicated to the proposition that human beings have the right to govern themselves and to live in freedom. The wisdom they displayed in crafting our Constitution continues to inspire people around the world who yearn for liberty and self-government.

The wisdom of the Founding Fathers in crafting the Second Amendment has been vindicated by more than two centuries of American experience. Their understanding that an armed citizenry was essential to both liberty and security has proven correct time and again, from the frontier period through two world wars to the present day.

The Founding Fathers' vision of citizen-soldiers has evolved with changing technology and circumstances, but the fundamental principle remains unchanged: a free people must retain the means to defend their freedom. Their wisdom in recognizing this truth and enshrining it in the Constitution represents one of the greatest achievements in the history of human government.

The debates of 1787 established principles that continue to guide America today. The Founding Fathers' understanding that liberty and security are not opposites but partners, that an armed citizenry is the foundation of both freedom and prosperity, and that the right to bear arms is essential to human dignity - these insights remain as relevant today as they were more than two centuries ago.

Their wisdom was not just intellectual but practical, not just theoretical but tested by experience. The men who crafted the Second Amendment had fought for liberty, governed free communities, and understood both the promise and the perils of self-government. Their legacy is a Constitution that has preserved American freedom longer than any other written constitution in history.

As we face the challenges of the 21st century, the wisdom of the Founding Fathers remains our guide. Their understanding that freedom requires vigilance, that liberty demands responsibility, and that the right to bear arms is essential to both - these truths are as relevant today as they were in 1787.

The Founding Fathers gave us not just a Constitution but a way of thinking about government, liberty, and human nature that continues to inspire people around the world. Their vision of America as a nation where the people retain the ultimate power, including the power of arms, remains the foundation of American exceptionalism and the hope of freedom-loving people everywhere.

The Second Amendment stands as a monument to their wisdom - a testament to their understanding that the price of liberty is eternal vigilance, and that the means of that vigilance must remain forever in the hands of the people themselves.

Chapter 6:
The Birth of the Second Amendment

The Second Amendment to the United States Constitution is one of the most debated and least understood provisions in the Bill of Rights. Its twenty-seven words have been the subject of countless court cases, scholarly articles, and political debates. But at its core, the Second Amendment is a simple and powerful statement about the right of the people to defend themselves, their families, and their country.

The Ratification Crisis: A Nation Demands Protection

The Second Amendment was born out of the compromise between the Federalists and the Anti-Federalists at the Constitutional Convention. But to understand its true significance, we must examine the passionate debates that raged across the thirteen states as Americans grappled with whether this new government would protect or threaten the liberties they had fought so hard to win.

The ratification of the Constitution was far from certain in 1787 and 1788. Across the thirteen states, passionate debates raged in state conventions, newspapers, and taverns about whether this new government would protect or threaten the liberties that Americans had fought so hard to win. At the center of these debates was a fundamental question: could the people trust their government to respect their rights without explicit constitutional protections?

The Anti-Federalists, who feared a powerful central government, demanded a Bill of Rights that would protect the rights of the people from government overreach. Led by men like Patrick Henry of Virginia, Robert Yates of New York, and George Clinton, they had lived through British tyranny and understood that governments, even well-intentioned ones, had a tendency to expand their power at the expense of individual liberty.

"Where are your landmarks, your boundaries of power?" Patrick Henry thundered during the Virginia ratifying convention. "The English history is full of such instances, and so is the history of all countries." Henry and his fellow Anti-Federalists understood that without explicit protections, the new federal government might follow the same path as the British Crown - gradually restricting the rights of the people until liberty was extinguished.

The Federalists, who believed that a Bill of Rights was unnecessary, eventually agreed to add one in order to secure the ratification of the Constitution. The question of military power was particularly contentious. The proposed Constitution gave the federal government the power to raise armies and maintain a navy, but it said nothing about the people's right to bear arms. For Americans who had just fought a war against a government that had tried to disarm them, this omission was deeply troubling.

The Pennsylvania Debates: Setting the Constitutional Stage

The Pennsylvania ratifying convention provided the first major test of public opinion on the Constitution and the need for a Bill of Rights. The Federalists, led by James Wilson, argued that a Bill of Rights was unnecessary because the federal government would have only those powers explicitly granted to it by the Constitution.

Wilson's argument was logical but failed to convince many Pennsylvanians who remembered how the British government had gradually expanded its power over the colonies. The Anti-Federalist minority in Pennsylvania, led by John Smilie and William Findley, demanded explicit protections for individual rights, including the right to bear arms.

"The people have a right to bear arms for the defense of themselves and their own state, or the United States, or for the purpose of killing game," declared the Pennsylvania Anti-Federalists in their dissenting opinion. This language would later influence Madison's drafting of the Second Amendment and established the principle that the right to bear arms served multiple purposes - self-defense, defense of the state, and hunting.

The Pennsylvania debates also revealed the deep connection between the right to bear arms and the militia system. Pennsylvania had a strong tradition of citizen-soldiers dating back to the colonial period, and many Pennsylvanians saw the militia as the best defense against both foreign invasion and domestic tyranny.

Madison's Masterful Drafting Process

James Madison, who is often called the "Father of the Constitution," was the primary author of the Bill of Rights. Madison approached the task of drafting the Bill of Rights with the same scholarly thoroughness that had characterized his preparation for the Constitutional Convention. Madison studied the constitutions and bills of rights of the various states, looking for language and concepts that had proven effective in protecting individual liberty.

His original draft of the Second Amendment was slightly different from the final version. It read: "The right of the people to keep and bear arms shall not be infringed; a well armed and well regulated militia being the best security of a free country: but no person religiously scrupulous of bearing arms shall be compelled to render military service in person."

Madison's original draft drew heavily on the Virginia Declaration of Rights, which had been authored by George Mason. But Madison made important changes that reflected his understanding of the federal system created by the Constitution. Where Mason's Virginia Declaration spoke of "a well-regulated militia, composed of the body of the people, trained to arms," Madison's draft emphasized that "a well armed and well regulated militia being the best security of a free country." This change reflected Madison's understanding that the militia was not just a state institution but a national one - a force that could defend the entire country against threats both foreign and domestic.

Madison's inclusion of the phrase "the right of the people to keep and bear arms shall not be infringed" was deliberate and significant. Madison could have written "the right of the militia" or "the right of the states," but he chose "the right of the people" - the same phrase used in the First and Fourth Amendments to protect individual rights.

The religious exemption clause in Madison's original draft - "but no person religiously scrupulous of bearing arms shall be compelled to render military service in person" - reflected his understanding that the right to bear arms was connected to militia service, but that this connection should not be used to force people to violate their religious beliefs.

The Congressional Debates: Refining the Language of Liberty

The draft was then debated and amended in the House and the Senate. When Madison introduced his proposed amendments to the House of Representatives on June 8, 1789, he sparked a debate that would clarify the meaning and purpose of what would become the Second Amendment. The congressional debates, recorded in the Annals of Congress, provide crucial insight into the Founders' intent.

Representative Elbridge Gerry of Massachusetts, who had refused to sign the Constitution because it lacked a Bill of Rights, strongly supported Madison's proposed amendment. Gerry understood that the right to bear arms was essential to the militia system and to individual liberty. "What, sir, is the use of a militia?" Gerry asked during the debates. "It is to prevent the establishment of a standing army, the bane of liberty."

Representative Jackson of Georgia worried that the religious exemption clause might be abused by people seeking to avoid military service. "No man can claim this indulgence of right," Jackson argued. "It may be a religious persuasion, but it is no natural right, and therefore ought to be left to the discretion of the Government."

The debate over the religious exemption revealed the tension between individual conscience and collective defense that would continue to influence American thinking about military service. Ultimately, the clause was removed from the final version, but the debate showed that the Founders understood the Second Amendment as protecting both individual rights and collective security.

Representative Benson of New York proposed changing Madison's language to make it clearer that the amendment protected individual rights. Benson suggested that the amendment should read: "A well regulated militia, composed of the body of the people, being the best security of a free state, the right of the people to keep and bear arms shall not be infringed."

This proposed change was significant because it emphasized that the militia was "composed of the body of the people" - not just a select group of soldiers but the entire citizenry. The change also made it clear that "the right of the people" was the operative clause, with the militia clause serving as an explanation of why this right was important.

The Senate's Final Touches

The Senate's consideration of the Second Amendment was conducted in secret, so we have no record of the debates. But we do know that the Senate made important changes to the language that had been approved by the House.

The final version, which was ratified in 1791, reads: "A well regulated Militia, being necessary to the security of a free State, the right of the people to keep and bear Arms, shall not be infringed."

The Senate's final version - was more concise than Madison's original draft but preserved its essential meaning. The Senate's decision to capitalize "Militia," "State," and "Arms" reflected the importance they placed on these concepts. The militia was not just any armed group but the constitutional institution that would defend American liberty. The "free State" was not just any political entity but the American republic that had been created by the Constitution. And "Arms" were not just any weapons but the tools of freedom that would enable the people to defend their liberty.

Understanding the Amendment's Revolutionary Language

The meaning of the Second Amendment has been the subject of intense debate for more than two hundred years. The debate has centered on two key phrases: "a well regulated Militia" and "the right of the people to keep and bear Arms."

The militia clause has been interpreted in two main ways. The collective rights theory holds that the Second Amendment protects the right of the states to maintain a militia, but that it does not protect the right of individuals to own firearms. The individual rights theory, on the other hand, holds that the Second Amendment protects the right of individuals to own firearms for self-defense and other purposes.

The "right of the people" clause has also been the subject of debate. Some have argued that "the people" refers to the people as a collective, while others have argued that it refers to individuals. The Supreme Court has now definitively ruled in favor of the individual rights interpretation, but the debate over the scope of that right continues to this day.

State Ratification: The People Speak

The ratification of the Bill of Rights by the states was not automatic. Each state had to consider whether these amendments were necessary and whether they adequately protected the rights of the people.

Virginia, Madison's home state, was among the first to ratify the Bill of Rights. The Virginia legislature understood that the Second Amendment reflected the state's own constitutional tradition and would protect the rights that Virginians had long cherished.

New York's ratification was more contentious. The state had a strong Anti-Federalist tradition, and many New Yorkers wanted even stronger protections for individual rights. But they ultimately concluded that the Second Amendment, combined with the other amendments in the Bill of Rights, provided adequate protection for the people's liberties.

Pennsylvania's ratification was particularly significant because the state had been the site of some of the most intense debates over the Constitution and the need for a Bill of Rights. The Pennsylvania legislature's approval of the Second Amendment vindicated the Anti-Federalists who had demanded explicit protections for the right to bear arms.

Contemporary Understanding: What Americans Thought

The ratification of the Second Amendment was greeted with widespread approval by the American people. Newspapers across the country praised the amendment as a crucial protection for individual liberty and collective security.

The Pennsylvania Gazette declared that the Second Amendment would ensure that "the people will always be armed, and can never be oppressed by a standing army." This understanding - that an armed citizenry was the best defense against military tyranny - was widely shared among Americans of all political persuasions.

The Massachusetts Centinel praised the amendment as a protection for "the natural right of resistance and self-preservation." This language reflected the understanding that the right to bear arms was not created by government but was a natural right that government existed to protect.

The Virginia Independent Chronicle emphasized that the Second Amendment would protect "the right of the people to keep and bear arms for their common defense." This interpretation recognized that the amendment protected both individual rights and collective security.

The Legal Framework: A Revolutionary System of Checks and Balances

The Second Amendment created a legal framework that balanced individual rights with collective security. The amendment recognized that the militia was "necessary to the security of a free State," but it protected "the right of the people to keep and bear Arms" as the means of ensuring that the militia would be effective.

This framework was revolutionary because it assumed that the people could be trusted with weapons and that an armed citizenry would strengthen rather than threaten the government. This was the opposite of the European model, where governments sought to monopolize military power and viewed armed citizens as a threat to order.

The amendment also created a system of checks and balances within the military sphere. The federal government could raise armies, but the people retained the right to bear arms. The states could organize militias, but the people's right to keep and bear arms could not be infringed. This system ensured that no single institution could monopolize military power.

The Philosophical Foundation: Natural Rights and Popular Sovereignty

The Second Amendment was grounded in the philosophical principles that had animated the American Revolution. The amendment assumed that the right to bear arms was a natural right that existed before government and that government existed to protect, not grant, this right.

This understanding was reflected in the amendment's language. The amendment did not say that government "grants" the right to bear arms or that the right exists "subject to regulation." Instead, it said that the right "shall not be infringed" - language that assumed the right already existed and that government's role was simply to respect it.

The amendment also reflected the principle of popular sovereignty - the idea that ultimate political power rested with the people. An armed citizenry was both a symbol and a guarantee of popular sovereignty, ensuring that the people would always retain the ultimate power to defend their liberty.

The International Context: America's Unique Experiment

The Second Amendment represented a radical departure from European practice and political theory. In Europe, the right to bear arms was typically restricted to the nobility and the military. The idea that ordinary citizens could be trusted with weapons was considered dangerous and revolutionary.

The American experiment in armed citizenship was watched with interest and alarm by European observers. Some, like the Marquis de Lafayette, saw it as a model for other nations seeking to establish free governments. Others, like British commentators, predicted that an armed American citizenry would lead to chaos and civil war.

The success of the American experiment would vindicate the Founders' faith in the people and demonstrate that an armed citizenry could coexist with ordered liberty. This success would inspire democratic movements around the world and establish America as the beacon of freedom for oppressed peoples everywhere.

The Cultural Impact: Shaping American Character

The Second Amendment helped shape American culture in ways that extended far beyond military affairs. The amendment encouraged self-reliance, individual responsibility, and respect for the rights of others - values that would become central to American character.

The amendment also fostered a culture of civic participation and community defense. Americans understood that their rights came with responsibilities and that the preservation of liberty required the active participation of citizens who were willing to defend their communities and their country.

This culture of armed citizenship would influence American literature, art, and popular culture for generations. From James Fenimore Cooper's frontier novels to the Western films of Hollywood, the image of the armed American defending liberty and justice would become an enduring symbol of American values.

A Living Amendment for All Generations

Despite the debates and the controversies, the Second Amendment remains a powerful symbol of American liberty. It is a reminder that the right to defend oneself is a fundamental human right, and that a well-armed citizenry is the ultimate check on the power of the state.

The Second Amendment was designed to be a living part of the Constitution, adapting to changing circumstances while preserving its essential purpose. The Founders understood that technology would change, that society would evolve, and that new threats to liberty would emerge. But they also understood that the fundamental principle - that free people must retain the means to defend their freedom - would remain constant.

The amendment's language was deliberately broad enough to encompass new technologies and new circumstances. The phrase "keep and bear Arms" was not limited to the muskets of 1791 but could include whatever weapons were necessary for the people to fulfill their role as the ultimate guardians of liberty.

The Enduring Legacy of Twenty-Seven Words

The Second Amendment stands as one of the greatest achievements of American constitutional law. It successfully balanced individual rights with collective security, created a system of checks and balances within the military sphere, and established principles that have preserved American liberty for more than two centuries.

The amendment's success has vindicated the Founders' faith in the American people and demonstrated that a free society can trust its citizens with the means of defending their liberty. This trust has been repaid by generations of Americans who have used their Second Amendment rights responsibly and who have defended their country with courage and honor.

The Second Amendment remains as relevant today as it was in 1791. In an age of new threats and new technologies, the amendment continues to serve its essential purpose: ensuring that the American people retain the means to defend their freedom against all enemies, foreign and domestic.

The twenty-seven words of the Second Amendment represent more than just a constitutional provision - they represent a philosophy of government, a theory of liberty, and a promise to future generations that America will always be the land of the free and the home of the brave.

Chapter 7:
1791 - The Year Freedom Was Secured

The year 1791 stands as one of the most remarkable years in the history of human liberty. It was a year when the young American republic, under the steady leadership of President George Washington, took bold steps to secure the blessings of freedom for generations to come. In this landmark year, the Bill of Rights was ratified, the Second Amendment became the law of the land, and the federal government faced its first major test of authority.

Picture, if you will, the America of 1791. George Washington, the hero of the Revolution, occupied the newly created office of President. The federal government was still in its infancy, operating out of the temporary capital of Philadelphia. The Constitution had been in effect for only two years, and many Americans were still uncertain about this new experiment in republican government.

It was in this atmosphere of hope and uncertainty that the Second Amendment was ratified on December 15, 1791, along with the other nine amendments that make up the Bill of Rights. The timing was perfect - the American people had just fought a war to secure their freedom, and they were determined to ensure that future generations would have the means to defend that freedom if necessary.

But 1791 was remarkable for another reason as well. It was the year that whiskey became the first domestic product ever to be taxed by the federal government. The Whiskey Tax, as it came to be known, was designed to help pay off the debts incurred during the Revolutionary War. But it also represented something more significant: it was the first time the new federal government had attempted to assert its authority over the daily lives of ordinary Americans.

The reaction to the Whiskey Tax was swift and fierce, particularly in western Pennsylvania, where whiskey was not just a beverage but a form of currency and a way of life. The farmers and distillers of the region saw the tax as an unfair burden and a threat to their livelihoods. They organized protests, they refused to pay the tax, and they used violence and intimidation to prevent its collection.

The Whiskey Rebellion, as it came to be known, was the first major test of the new federal government's authority. President Washington, who understood that the survival of the republic depended on the government's ability to enforce its laws, called up the militia to suppress the rebellion. It was a dramatic moment - the same militias that had fought for independence were now being called upon to enforce the authority of the government they had helped to create.

The suppression of the Whiskey Rebellion was a victory for the rule of law and the authority of the federal government. But it was also a victory for the Second Amendment and the principle of an armed citizenry. The militias that marched on western Pennsylvania were composed of ordinary citizens who had answered their country's call. They were living proof that the Second Amendment was not just words on paper, but a practical reality that could be called upon in times of crisis.

The year 1791 also saw the beginning of westward expansion on a grand scale. The frontier beckoned to thousands of Americans who were eager to make new lives for themselves in the vast wilderness beyond the Appalachian Mountains. These pioneers carried with them their firearms, their determination, and their belief in the American dream. They would face countless challenges in the years to come - hostile weather, difficult terrain, and conflicts with Native American tribes - but they would meet these challenges with courage and resolve.

The America of 1791 was a nation on the move, a nation full of energy and optimism. It was a nation that had just secured its freedom and was determined to make the most of it. The Second Amendment was a crucial part of that freedom, a guarantee that the American people would always have the means to defend themselves, their families, and their country.

Looking back on 1791 from our vantage point in the 21st century, we can see it as a pivotal year in the history of human liberty. It was the year when the American people, through their elected representatives, declared that the right to keep and bear arms was a fundamental human right that could not be infringed. It was the year when the federal government proved that it could enforce its laws while still respecting the rights of its citizens. And it was the year when the American experiment in republican government took a giant step forward toward becoming the beacon of freedom that it is today.

The Code of Honor: Dueling in Early America

In the early years of the American republic, firearms played a unique and fascinating role in the culture of honor that defined gentlemen's society. The practice of dueling, while controversial even in its time, represented a formal system by which men of standing settled disputes of honor through armed combat. This tradition, imported from Europe but adapted to American circumstances, provides a remarkable window into how deeply firearms were embedded in the social fabric of early America.

The culture of dueling in America reached its peak in the decades following the Revolution, precisely when the Second Amendment was being written and ratified. For the Founding Fathers and their contemporaries, the ability to defend one's honor with arms was considered an essential right of free men. The duel was seen not as mere violence, but as a civilized alternative to brawling or assassination - a way for gentlemen to settle their differences according to established rules and codes of conduct.

The most famous duel in American history took place on July 11, 1804, when Alexander Hamilton, the brilliant first Secretary of the Treasury, faced Aaron Burr, the sitting Vice President of the United States, on the dueling grounds of Weehawken, New Jersey. The confrontation was the culmination of years of political and personal animosity between two of the most prominent figures in early American politics.

The Hamilton-Burr duel began with a series of newspaper articles in which Hamilton had made disparaging remarks about Burr's character and fitness for office. When Burr demanded satisfaction, Hamilton found himself trapped by the code of honor that governed gentlemen's conduct. To refuse the challenge would have meant social and political ruin, while accepting it meant risking his life for the sake of his reputation.

The duel was conducted according to the formal rules known as the Code Duello, which had been refined over centuries of European practice. Each man chose a "second" - a trusted friend who would handle the arrangements and ensure that the rules were followed. Hamilton's second was Nathaniel Pendleton, while Burr's was William P. Van Ness. The weapons were a matched pair of .56 caliber smoothbore pistols, and the distance was set at ten paces.

On that fateful morning, the two men met at dawn on the dueling ground. They stood back to back, walked ten paces, turned, and fired. Hamilton's shot went wide, striking a tree branch twelve feet above Burr's head. Burr's shot struck Hamilton in the lower abdomen, inflicting a mortal wound. Hamilton died the next day, and Burr, though technically the victor, found his political career destroyed by the public outcry that followed.

The Hamilton-Burr duel shocked the nation and marked the beginning of the end for dueling as an accepted practice among American gentlemen. But it also illustrated the central role that firearms played in the culture of the early republic. Both Hamilton and Burr were skilled marksmen who understood the technical aspects of their weapons. The fact that Hamilton's shot went wide was likely intentional - he had reportedly told his second that he intended to "throw away" his shot, a practice known as "deloping" that allowed a duelist to satisfy honor without taking his opponent's life.

Perhaps no American was more associated with dueling than Andrew Jackson, the future seventh President of the United States. Jackson fought numerous duels throughout his life, earning a reputation as one of the most dangerous men in America. His most famous duel took place in 1806 against Charles Dickinson, who was considered one of the best shots in Tennessee.

The Jackson-Dickinson duel arose from a dispute over a horse race and some insulting remarks about Jackson's wife, Rachel. Dickinson was known for his quick draw and deadly accuracy, and many observers expected him to kill Jackson easily. The duel was fought with pistols at twenty-four feet, and Dickinson was given the honor of firing first.

Dickinson's shot struck Jackson in the chest, breaking two ribs and lodging near his heart. But Jackson, showing incredible courage and determination, remained standing and took careful aim. His shot struck Dickinson in the abdomen, inflicting a mortal wound. Dickinson died that evening, while Jackson carried the bullet in his chest for the rest of his life.

Jackson's victory over Dickinson enhanced his reputation as a man not to be trifled with, but it also demonstrated the importance of mental toughness and marksmanship skills in dueling. Jackson understood that in a duel, as in war, the man who could remain calm under pressure and shoot accurately had the best chance of survival.

The technical aspects of dueling were quite sophisticated. The weapons used were typically smoothbore flintlock pistols, often made in matched pairs by skilled gunsmiths. These pistols were designed specifically for dueling, with features that ensured fairness and accuracy. They usually had hair triggers for quick firing, and they were carefully balanced for precise aim.

The Code Duello established detailed rules for how duels should be conducted. The challenged party had the right to choose weapons and conditions, while the challenger had the right to choose the time and place. Seconds played a crucial role, not just in making arrangements but in attempting to resolve the dispute without bloodshed. Many potential duels were settled through the intervention of seconds who found ways for both parties to maintain their honor without fighting.

There were several different formats for duels. The most common was the "walk and turn" method, where the duelists stood back to back, walked a predetermined number of paces, turned, and fired on command. Another format involved the duelists standing at a fixed distance and firing simultaneously on a signal. Some duels were fought "at will," where the duelists could fire whenever they chose after the signal was given.

The culture of dueling was not limited to politicians and military officers. Merchants, lawyers, doctors, and other professional men all participated in this ritual of honor. Newspapers regularly reported on duels, and the public followed them with great interest. A man's reputation as a duelist could enhance his standing in society, while a refusal to duel could destroy his social and professional prospects.

Dueling also played a role in the development of American marksmanship traditions. Men who might be called upon to defend their honor needed to be skilled with firearms, and this created a culture of practice and training that extended far beyond the dueling ground. Shooting clubs and marksmanship competitions became popular, and the skills developed in these activities served the nation well in times of war.

The practice of dueling began to decline in the 1830s and 1840s as American society became more democratic and less hierarchical. The rise of the common man and the decline of aristocratic pretensions made the elaborate rituals of honor seem increasingly outdated. Religious opposition to dueling also grew stronger, and many states passed laws making dueling illegal.

But the legacy of dueling culture lived on in American attitudes toward firearms and personal honor. The idea that a free man should be able to defend himself and his reputation with arms became deeply embedded in American culture. The skills and traditions developed in the dueling era contributed to the marksmanship excellence that would characterize American military forces in future conflicts.

The dueling culture of early America also reinforced the principles that would later be enshrined in the Second Amendment. The right to keep and bear arms was seen not just as a collective right related to militia service, but as an individual right connected to personal honor and self-defense. The Founding Fathers who wrote and ratified the Second Amendment lived in a world where the ability to defend oneself with arms was considered an essential attribute of free citizenship.

Today, while we no longer settle disputes through formal combat, the principles underlying the dueling culture remain relevant. The idea that free people should have the means to defend themselves, their families, and their honor continues to resonate in American society. The Second Amendment protects not just our right to own firearms, but our right to maintain the dignity and independence that have always been the hallmarks of American citizenship.

The dueling culture of early America reminds us that the right to keep and bear arms has deep roots in American history and culture. It was not just about hunting or militia service, but about the fundamental right of free people to defend themselves and their honor. While the formal practice of dueling has long since disappeared, the spirit that animated it - the belief that free people should never be defenseless - lives on in the Second Amendment and in the hearts of Americans who understand that freedom is not free, and that sometimes it must be defended with force.

> *"The duel was never truly about death; it was about dignity —*
> *a man's final appeal when all other words failed."*

Chapter 8:
The Civil War Era - Industry vs. Ingenuity

The Civil War era marked a revolutionary period in American firearms technology and manufacturing that would establish the United States as the world leader in innovation and industrial might. This was the time when American ingenuity and the spirit of free enterprise combined to create some of the most advanced weapons systems the world had ever seen.

The massive mobilization effort required to arm the Union and Confederate forces sparked an unprecedented boom in American manufacturing. Companies like Colt, Remington, and Winchester expanded their operations dramatically, employing thousands of workers and pioneering new production techniques that would later be applied to peacetime industries. The Springfield Armory became a model of efficiency and precision manufacturing that impressed visitors from around the world.

The Union Arsenal: Industrial Might Meets Innovation

The Union's victory in the Civil War was built not just on superior numbers and resources, but on the technological superiority of American-manufactured firearms. Northern factories, led by the Springfield Armory and private manufacturers like Colt and Remington, produced weapons that gave Union soldiers decisive advantages on the battlefield.

The Springfield Model 1861: The Backbone of Union Victory

The Springfield Model 1861 rifle-musket became the standard infantry weapon of the Union Army, with over 1.5 million produced during the war. This .58 caliber muzzle-loading rifle represented the pinnacle of traditional firearms technology, combining accuracy, reliability, and ease of manufacture.

The Springfield's three-band barrel design and precision rifling allowed soldiers to hit targets accurately at ranges up to 500 yards - a revolutionary improvement over the smooth-bore muskets of previous wars. The weapon used the innovative Minié ball, a conical bullet that expanded when fired to grip the rifling, providing both accuracy and ease of loading.

Union soldiers praised the Springfield for its reliability and accuracy. Private John Billings of the 10th Massachusetts Battery wrote, "Our Springfield rifles never failed us. In rain or shine, in the mud of Virginia or the dust of Georgia, they fired true every time." This reliability gave Union forces confidence in their equipment and contributed significantly to Northern morale.

The Springfield Armory's production methods became a model for American manufacturing. The use of interchangeable parts, precision machinery, and quality control systems allowed the armory to produce thousands of identical rifles that could be maintained and repaired in the field using standardized components.

Revolutionary Repeating Rifles: Changing the Face of Warfare

This period saw the introduction of revolutionary firearms that showcased American innovation. The Spencer repeating rifle, invented by Christopher Spencer, could fire seven rounds without reloading - a tremendous advantage over single-shot weapons. This lever-action rifle represented a quantum leap in firearms technology that gave Union cavalry and select infantry units an overwhelming advantage.

The Spencer's rate of fire was revolutionary - a trained soldier could fire 20 aimed rounds per minute, compared to 3 rounds per minute with a muzzle-loading rifle. This firepower advantage was so significant that Confederate soldiers called it "that damned Yankee rifle you load on Sunday and shoot all week."

President Lincoln himself test-fired the Spencer on the White House lawn in August 1863, hitting a target at 40 yards with several shots. Impressed by the weapon's performance, Lincoln ordered the War Department to purchase Spencer rifles for Union cavalry units. By war's end, over 200,000 Spencer rifles and carbines had been delivered to Union forces.

The Henry rifle, with its distinctive brass frame, became known as "the gun you could load on Sunday and shoot all week." This lever-action rifle held 15 rounds of .44 caliber ammunition in a tubular magazine beneath the barrel, giving it even greater firepower than the Spencer. While the Henry was primarily purchased by individual soldiers rather than issued by the government, it became legendary among Union troops who could afford to buy one.

The 1st District of Columbia Cavalry was one of the few units officially equipped with Henry rifles. During the 1864 Shenandoah Valley Campaign, the regiment's Henrys proved devastatingly effective against Confederate cavalry, with one officer reporting, "The enemy could not understand how we could fire so rapidly and accurately. They thought we had some new form of artillery."

Colt Revolvers: The Union's Sidearm of Choice

Samuel Colt's revolving pistols became the standard sidearm for Union cavalry and officers. The Colt Army Model 1860, chambered in .44 caliber, and the Navy Model 1851, in .36 caliber, provided reliable, rapid-fire capability that was essential for mounted combat.

The Colt Army revolver's six-shot capacity and quick reloading made it ideal for cavalry charges and close-quarters combat. Union cavalry commander General Philip Sheridan equipped his entire command with Colt revolvers, stating, "A cavalryman with a Colt is worth three men with sabers."

The precision manufacturing at Colt's Hartford factory ensured that every revolver met exacting standards. The company's use of interchangeable parts meant that damaged revolvers could be quickly repaired in the field, maintaining unit effectiveness even during extended campaigns.

Confederate Ingenuity: Making Do with Less

The Confederacy faced enormous challenges in arming its forces, lacking the industrial infrastructure of the North. However, Southern ingenuity and determination led to remarkable innovations and adaptations that kept Confederate forces competitive throughout the war.

The Richmond Rifle-Musket: Southern Manufacturing Excellence

The Richmond Armory, established in captured machinery from the Harpers Ferry Arsenal, became the Confederacy's primary source of infantry weapons. The Richmond rifle-musket, closely modeled on the U.S. Model 1855, proved that Southern manufacturers could produce weapons equal in quality to their Northern counterparts.

Despite shortages of raw materials and skilled workers, the Richmond Armory produced over 300,000 rifle-muskets during the war. These weapons were highly regarded by Confederate soldiers for their accuracy and reliability. General Robert E. Lee specifically praised the Richmond rifles, noting that they "served our cause with distinction and honor."

The armory's success demonstrated Southern industrial capability and the dedication of Confederate workers. Master armorer James Burton, who had previously worked at Harpers Ferry, brought his expertise to Richmond and established production methods that rivaled those of Northern factories.

Confederate Innovation Under Pressure

The Confederacy's lack of access to Colt revolvers led to remarkable innovation in handgun design and manufacturing. The Griswold & Gunnison revolver, manufactured in Georgia, became one of the most successful Confederate handguns. Using brass frames to conserve steel, these revolvers were reliable and accurate, earning praise from Confederate cavalry units.

Lemat revolvers, designed by Dr. Jean Alexandre LeMat of New Orleans, featured a unique design with a nine-shot cylinder and a separate shotgun barrel. This innovative weapon provided Confederate officers with exceptional firepower, with General J.E.B. Stuart and other cavalry commanders carrying LeMat revolvers throughout the war.

The British-made Whitworth rifle became the weapon of choice for Confederate sharpshooters. This hexagonal-bore rifle was incredibly accurate, capable of hitting targets at ranges exceeding 1,000 yards. At the Battle of Spotsylvania, Confederate marksman Ben Powell used a Whitworth rifle to kill Union General John Sedgwick at a range of over 800 yards, demonstrating the weapon's exceptional accuracy.

Artillery Revolution: The Big Guns of Innovation

The famous Gatling gun, invented by Dr. Richard Gatling, was one of the first successful machine guns. Gatling actually hoped his invention would reduce casualties by allowing smaller forces to be more effective, thus shortening conflicts. The Gatling gun's hand-cranked mechanism could fire up to 200 rounds per minute, providing firepower equivalent to dozens of riflemen.

The Parrott rifle, designed by Robert Parker Parrott at the West Point Foundry, became the Union's most successful rifled artillery piece. These guns provided Union forces with superior range and accuracy, with their innovative wrought-iron reinforcing bands allowing them to withstand the pressures of rifled projectiles.

The 12-pounder Napoleon cannon, used by both sides, became the most popular artillery piece of the war. This reliable bronze cannon could fire solid shot, explosive shells, and canister rounds, making it versatile enough for any battlefield situation.

The Armed Citizenry: Personal Weapons and Individual Initiative

The war also demonstrated the importance of an armed citizenry in defending their homes and communities. Throughout the conflict, civilians on both sides used their personal firearms to protect their families and property. This reinforced the wisdom of the Founding Fathers in ensuring that Americans would always have the right to keep and bear arms.

Many Union and Confederate soldiers supplemented their issued weapons with personal firearms, often weapons that were superior to government-issued arms. These personal weapons reflected the strong American tradition of civilian marksmanship and gun ownership.

The famous Confederate sniper "California Joe" Milner carried a custom-built target rifle that he had owned before the war. His exceptional marksmanship with this personal weapon made him one of the most feared snipers in the Confederate army. Similarly, Union sharpshooter Truman Head brought his own target rifle to war and used it to great effect in the Berdan Sharpshooters.

While the war's outcome wasn't determined by any single weapon, these innovations showed how American inventors were constantly working to give their side technological advantages. The combination of industrial might, individual innovation, and the skills of an armed citizenry proved decisive in preserving the Union.

Manufacturing Excellence: Setting Global Standards

Perhaps most importantly, the Civil War era established American firearms manufacturers as the finest in the world. The precision, reliability, and innovation of American-made weapons became legendary. European armies began purchasing American firearms, and American gunmakers started exporting their products globally. This industrial success story was built on the foundation of American freedom and the right to keep and bear arms.

The Springfield Armory pioneered the use of precision gauges and inspection systems that ensured every rifle met exact specifications. These quality control methods were later adopted by civilian manufacturers and contributed to the reputation of American-made products worldwide.

Private manufacturers like Colt, Remington, and Winchester expanded their facilities and developed new production techniques to meet wartime demand. These innovations allowed them to dominate civilian markets after the war and establish American firearms as the finest in the world.

The Peaceful Dividend: From War to Prosperity

The post-war period saw these same manufacturers turn their expertise toward civilian markets, producing hunting rifles, target guns, and personal defense weapons that would serve American families for generations. The technological advances made during the war years continued to benefit civilian shooters, hunters, and sportsmen long after the conflict ended.

The Henry rifle's impact extended beyond the Civil War. Many veterans carried their rifles west after the war, where the weapon's reliability and firepower made it ideal for frontier conditions. This civilian use demonstrated how military innovations could benefit peacetime applications.

The precision manufacturing techniques that produced military rifles were applied to hunting rifles, target guns, and personal defense weapons. The same commitment to quality, innovation, and reliability that characterized Civil War-era weapons became the hallmark of American-made firearms.

A Legacy of Excellence

The Civil War era proved that American industry, driven by free enterprise and innovation, could meet any challenge. The same spirit that created the finest military weapons in the world also produced the finest civilian firearms, establishing a tradition of excellence that continues to this day. This was American manufacturing at its finest - efficient, innovative, and dedicated to producing the highest quality products in the world.

The technological advances made during the Civil War established American firearms manufacturers as world leaders in innovation and quality. The precision, reliability, and effectiveness of American weapons impressed military observers from around the globe, leading to international recognition and export opportunities that demonstrated the benefits of free enterprise and innovation.

The weapons that helped preserve the Union and end slavery were products of American ingenuity, craftsmanship, and the fundamental right to keep and bear arms that had made such innovation possible. This period established traditions of excellence in American firearms manufacturing that continue today, ensuring that the legacy of this remarkable era continues to serve American freedom and security.

The Civil War era demonstrated that when free people are allowed to innovate, create, and compete, they can achieve remarkable things. The firearms industry that emerged from this conflict would continue to serve American hunters, sportsmen, and defenders of freedom for generations to come, proving that the Second Amendment was not just about the right to bear arms, but about the right to excel, innovate, and lead the world in the tools of freedom.

"The efficiency of this arm is beyond anything yet produced. One man armed with a repeating rifle is worth a dozen with the old muzzle-loader."
— Gen. Ulysses S. Grant
(on the Henry and Spencer repeating rifles introduced during the war)

Chapter 9:
The Fight for Universal Freedom

The end of the Civil War brought not just victory for the Union, but the promise of freedom for all Americans. The story of how the Second Amendment became a tool for protecting the newly freed slaves is one of the most inspiring chapters in American history - a testament to how the right to keep and bear arms serves as the ultimate guarantor of liberty for all people.

The Thirteenth Amendment abolished slavery, but it was the Fourteenth Amendment and the Civil Rights Act of 1866 that truly secured the blessings of liberty for African Americans. And at the heart of these protections was the recognition that the right to keep and bear arms was essential for all free people.

The Civil Rights Act of 1866 was revolutionary in its scope and vision. It declared that all persons born in the United States were citizens, and it guaranteed all citizens "the same right in every State and Territory to make and enforce contracts, to sue, be parties, give evidence, and to the full and equal benefit of all laws and proceedings for the security of persons and property as is enjoyed by white citizens, and shall be subject to like punishment, pains, penalties, taxes, licenses, and exactions of every kind, and to no other."

But perhaps most importantly for our story, the Act specifically protected the right of all citizens to keep and bear arms. This was no accident - the Republican Congress understood that an unarmed people could never be truly free. They had seen how attempts to disarm African Americans were used as tools of oppression, and they were determined to ensure that all Americans would have the means to defend themselves and their families.

The heroes of this era were not just the politicians who passed these laws, but the ordinary African Americans who exercised their newly secured rights. Take, for example, the story of Robert Smalls, a former slave who became a Civil War hero, a successful businessman, and a five-term Congressman from South Carolina. Smalls understood that freedom meant more than just the absence of chains - it meant the ability to defend oneself and one's community.

Or consider the story of the Deacons for Defense and Justice, an armed African American self-defense organization that protected civil rights workers during the 1960s. These brave men understood what the Founding Fathers had understood two centuries earlier - that the right to keep and bear arms is the right that protects all other rights.

The period of Reconstruction was not without its challenges, of course. There were those who sought to deny African Americans their newly won rights, and there were violent groups like the Ku Klux Klan that used terror and intimidation to try to turn back the clock. But the response of the federal government was swift and decisive. The Enforcement Acts of 1870 and 1871 gave the federal government the power to prosecute those who would deny citizens their constitutional rights, including the right to keep and bear arms.

The story of Reconstruction is ultimately a story of triumph - the triumph of the American ideals of freedom and equality over the forces of oppression and tyranny. It is a story that shows how the Second Amendment serves not just as a protection for the majority, but as a shield for the vulnerable and the oppressed.

This period also saw the rise of some of America's most skilled marksmen and women, regardless of race. The Buffalo Soldiers, African American cavalry regiments, became legendary for their courage and skill with firearms on the Western frontier. Their marksmanship and discipline earned them the respect of both their comrades and their enemies.

The Buffalo Soldiers: Heroes of the Frontier

Among the most heroic and skilled marksmen of the post-Civil War era were the Buffalo Soldiers - the African American cavalry and infantry regiments that served with distinction on the Western frontier. These remarkable men proved that courage, skill, and dedication to duty know no color, and their service helped secure the American West while earning them a place among the greatest soldiers in American history.

The Buffalo Soldiers were formed in 1866 when Congress authorized the creation of six all-black regiments: the 9th and 10th Cavalry Regiments and the 38th, 39th, 40th, and 41st Infantry Regiments (later consolidated into the 24th and 25th Infantry). These units were commanded by white officers, but the enlisted men were all African Americans, many of them Civil War veterans who had proven their valor in the fight to preserve the Union.

The name "Buffalo Soldiers" was given to these troops by the Native

American tribes they encountered on the frontier. Far from being an insult, this was a mark of the highest respect. The Plains Indians revered the buffalo as a sacred animal, embodying strength, courage, and endurance. When they called these black cavalrymen "Buffalo Soldiers," they were acknowledging their fighting spirit and their tenacity in battle.

The Buffalo Soldiers served in some of the most challenging and dangerous assignments in the American military. They were stationed at remote frontier posts, often in harsh and unforgiving terrain, where they faced not only hostile Native American tribes but also extreme weather, disease, and the constant threat of attack. Despite these challenges, they maintained the highest standards of military discipline and professionalism.

One of the most remarkable aspects of the Buffalo Soldiers was their exceptional marksmanship. These men understood that on the frontier, accuracy with firearms could mean the difference between life and death, not just for themselves but for the settlers and travelers they were sworn to protect. They practiced constantly with their weapons, becoming some of the finest shots in the entire U.S. Army.

The standard weapon of the Buffalo Soldier cavalry was the Springfield Model 1873 carbine, a single-shot breech-loading rifle that was reliable and accurate in the hands of a skilled marksman. The infantry units carried the full-length Springfield rifle. These weapons required careful maintenance in the harsh conditions of the frontier, and the Buffalo Soldiers became experts at keeping their firearms in perfect working condition despite dust, sand, and extreme temperatures.

Sergeant Emanuel Stance of the 9th Cavalry was one of the first Buffalo Soldiers to earn the Medal of Honor, America's highest military decoration. In May 1870, Stance led a small detachment in pursuit of Apache raiders who had stolen horses from a ranch near Fort McKavett, Texas. When the soldiers caught up with the raiders, Stance's expert marksmanship and tactical leadership enabled his small force to defeat a much larger group of Apache warriors and recover the stolen horses.

The citation for Stance's Medal of Honor praised his "gallant conduct during campaigns and engagements with Indians." But it was his skill with firearms that made his heroism possible. Stance could hit targets at ranges that amazed his fellow soldiers, and his ability to place accurate fire under combat conditions saved lives and completed missions that might otherwise have failed.

Another legendary Buffalo Soldier was Sergeant William McBryar of the 10th Cavalry, who earned his Medal of Honor during the Apache Wars in Arizona. McBryar's unit was pursuing a band of Apache raiders when they were ambushed in a narrow canyon. The situation looked hopeless - the soldiers were outnumbered and pinned down by accurate rifle fire from the canyon walls above.

But McBryar's exceptional marksmanship turned the tide of battle. Using his Springfield carbine, he began picking off the Apache snipers one by one, his shots echoing through the canyon as each bullet found its mark. His accurate fire not only eliminated the immediate threat but also demoralized the remaining Apache warriors, who withdrew rather than face this deadly marksman. McBryar's heroism saved his entire unit and allowed them to complete their mission.

The Buffalo Soldiers also played a crucial role in protecting the builders of the transcontinental railroad. As the railroad pushed westward across the Great Plains, construction crews faced constant attacks from Native American war parties who saw the "iron horse" as a threat to their way of life. The Buffalo Soldiers provided security for these crews, using their marksmanship skills to drive off attackers and keep the railroad construction on schedule.

One of the most famous incidents occurred in 1867 when a detachment of the 10th Cavalry was escorting a railroad survey party in Kansas. The group was attacked by a large war party of Cheyenne warriors, who had hoped to overwhelm the small military escort. But the Buffalo Soldiers' disciplined rifle fire and tactical expertise turned what should have been a massacre into a victory for the cavalry.

The soldiers formed a defensive perimeter and used their Springfield carbines to devastating effect. Their accurate, sustained fire kept the Cheyenne warriors at a distance, preventing them from using their superior numbers to overrun the position. After several hours of fighting, the war party withdrew, having suffered heavy casualties while inflicting minimal losses on the Buffalo Soldiers.

The Buffalo Soldiers' reputation for marksmanship was not limited to combat situations. They regularly participated in shooting competitions with other Army units, and they consistently performed at the highest levels. Their success in these competitions was a source of great pride for the regiments and helped to break down racial barriers within the military.

In 1892, the 25th Infantry Regiment won the Army's prestigious marksmanship competition, defeating teams from white regiments that had previously dominated the contest. This victory was particularly significant because it demonstrated that the Buffalo Soldiers were not just brave fighters but also technically proficient soldiers who could excel in any military skill.

The Buffalo Soldiers also served as some of America's first park rangers, protecting the newly created national parks in the West. They patrolled Yellowstone and Sequoia National Parks, using their outdoor skills and marksmanship abilities to protect wildlife from poachers and to assist visitors who found themselves in dangerous situations.

Their service in the national parks was particularly challenging because they had to balance their law enforcement duties with the need to maintain good relations with civilian visitors, some of whom harbored racial prejudices. Despite these challenges, the Buffalo Soldiers performed their duties with professionalism and distinction, helping to establish the traditions of the National Park Service.

The technical skills of the Buffalo Soldiers extended beyond marksmanship to include horsemanship, scouting, and survival in harsh environments. They became expert trackers who could follow trails across terrain that would challenge even experienced frontiersmen. Their ability to live off the land and operate independently for extended periods made them invaluable for long-range patrols and reconnaissance missions.

The Buffalo Soldiers also played an important role in the Indian Wars, though their relationship with Native American tribes was complex. While they fought against hostile war parties, they also developed a grudging respect for their opponents, who recognized the Buffalo Soldiers as worthy adversaries. This mutual respect was based partly on the soldiers' fighting skills and partly on their understanding of the harsh realities of frontier life.

Many Buffalo Soldiers served multiple enlistments, making the Army their career and becoming some of the most experienced soldiers on the frontier. Their knowledge of tactics, terrain, and enemy capabilities made them invaluable to their commanders, and their steady presence helped to maintain discipline and morale in the ranks.

The legacy of the Buffalo Soldiers extends far beyond their military service. They proved that African Americans could serve with distinction in any capacity, breaking down barriers and paving the way for future generations. Their marksmanship skills and military professionalism helped to establish standards that would influence the U.S. Army for decades to come.

The Buffalo Soldiers also demonstrated the importance of the Second Amendment for all Americans. Their right to keep and bear arms was not just a military necessity but a fundamental aspect of their citizenship. After their military service, many Buffalo Soldiers settled in the West, where they used their firearms skills for hunting, self-defense, and sport shooting.

Today, the Buffalo Soldiers are remembered as heroes who served their country with honor despite facing discrimination and prejudice. Their story reminds us that the right to keep and bear arms has always been essential for protecting freedom and ensuring that all Americans can defend themselves and their communities. The Buffalo Soldiers proved that in the hands of skilled and dedicated Americans, firearms are instruments of justice and protection, tools that help to build and defend civilization rather than destroy it.

The legacy of this era is clear: the Second Amendment is not just about hunting or sport shooting, though it protects those activities. It is not just about collecting firearms, though it protects that right as well. At its core, the Second Amendment is about human dignity and the fundamental right of all people to defend themselves, their families, and their communities from those who would do them harm.

The fight for universal freedom that began during Reconstruction continues to this day. Every time a law-abiding citizen uses a firearm to defend themselves or their family, they are exercising the same right that the heroes of Reconstruction fought to secure. Every time we stand up for the Second Amendment, we are standing up for the principle that all people, regardless of race, religion, or background, have the right to defend themselves and their loved ones.

This is the true legacy of the post-Civil War era - not division and conflict, but the expansion of freedom and the recognition that the right to keep and bear arms is truly a right for all Americans.

Chapter 10:
The Wild West - Where Legends Were Born

The Wild West represents one of America's most exciting and adventurous chapters, a time when brave men and women carved civilization out of the wilderness with courage, determination, and yes, firearms. This was the era that gave birth to some of America's most colorful legends and showed the world what American spirit could accomplish.

The frontier was a place where a person's character mattered more than their pedigree, where quick thinking and steady nerves could make the difference between life and death. It was here that the American ideals of self-reliance and individual responsibility were tested and proven in the crucible of the untamed West.

Wild Bill Hickok stands as one of the most fascinating figures of this era. James Butler Hickok earned his nickname through his incredible marksmanship and his service as a Union scout during the Civil War. His legendary quick-draw skills were not just Hollywood fiction - witnesses recorded that he could draw and fire two Navy Colt revolvers faster than most men could draw one. Wild Bill served as a lawman in some of the toughest towns on the frontier, bringing order to places where chaos had reigned.

Wild Bill Hickok: The Prince of Pistoleers

James Butler Hickok was born in 1837 in Homer, Illinois, but he would become known to the world as "Wild Bill," one of the most legendary gunfighters and lawmen in American history. His story is one of courage, skill, and the kind of larger-than-life adventures that could only happen on the American frontier. Wild Bill represented the best of the frontier spirit - a man who stood for justice, protected the innocent, and never backed down from a fight when he was in the right.

Bill's path to legend began early. As a young man, he was already known for his exceptional marksmanship and his fearless nature. He stood six feet tall with flowing hair and a mustache, cutting an impressive figure that commanded respect wherever he went. But it was his skill with firearms that truly set him apart from other men of his time.

Wild Bill's reputation was built on more than just his ability to shoot accurately - he was lightning fast on the draw. Witnesses described his technique as almost supernatural. He carried two Navy Colt .36 caliber revolvers in a red sash around his waist, butts forward in the cavalry style. When trouble started, Bill could cross-draw both pistols simultaneously and have them firing before most men could clear leather with one gun. This wasn't just showmanship - it was a survival skill that kept him alive in some of the most dangerous situations imaginable.

His first taste of real adventure came in 1861 when he was working as a stagecoach driver in Kansas. Bill got into a dispute with David McCanles over a woman and some business dealings. The confrontation escalated, and McCanles came to the station with two other men, apparently intent on violence. What happened next became the stuff of legend. Bill shot and killed McCanles and wounded the other two men, who were finished off by other station employees. This was Bill's first recorded gunfight, and it established his reputation as a man not to be trifled with.

When the Civil War broke out, Wild Bill found his calling as a Union scout and spy. His knowledge of the frontier, his shooting skills, and his courage made him invaluable to the Union Army. He operated behind Confederate lines, gathering intelligence and disrupting enemy operations. This was dangerous work that required not just bravery but also quick thinking and the ability to talk his way out of trouble when stealth failed.

One of Bill's most famous wartime exploits occurred when he was captured by Confederate forces. Using his wits and his charm, he convinced his captors that he was actually a Confederate sympathizer who had been forced to work for the Union. He not only talked his way to freedom but also managed to gather valuable intelligence about Confederate troop movements before making his escape. Stories like this made Wild Bill a legend among Union forces and earned him the respect of his commanders.

After the war, Bill's reputation as a gunfighter continued to grow. In 1865, he faced Dave Tutt in what many consider the first true quick-draw duel in the American West. The two men had been friends but had fallen out over gambling debts and a woman. They met in the town square of Springfield, Missouri, at about 75 yards apart - an enormous distance for a pistol duel.

The confrontation was like something out of a Western movie, except it was real. The two men faced each other in the street, hands hovering over their guns. Tutt drew first, but Bill was faster and more accurate. Both men fired almost simultaneously, but Tutt's shot went wide while Bill's bullet struck Tutt in the heart, killing him instantly. The shot was so remarkable - a perfect hit at 75 yards with a handgun - that it became legendary throughout the frontier.

Wild Bill's career as a lawman began in earnest after the war. He served as a deputy U.S. Marshal and later as sheriff of Ellis County, Kansas, which included the wild cow town of Hays City. This was one of the toughest assignments in law enforcement - Hays City was filled with cowboys, gamblers, and outlaws, and violence was a daily occurrence.

Bill brought order to Hays City through a combination of courage, skill, and psychological warfare. His reputation preceded him, and many troublemakers thought twice before causing problems in a town where Wild Bill Hickok was the law. But when violence did occur, Bill was ready for it. He killed several men in the line of duty, always in fair fights and always in defense of law and order.

Perhaps Bill's most famous assignment was as marshal of Abilene, Kansas, in 1871. Abilene was the end of the Chisholm Trail, where Texas cowboys drove their cattle to be shipped east by railroad. The town was wild and lawless, with saloons, gambling halls, and brothels operating around the clock. Previous marshals had either been killed or had fled in fear.

Wild Bill transformed Abilene into a relatively peaceful town through his presence and his reputation. He didn't have to kill many men because most troublemakers knew better than to challenge him. His mere presence on the street was enough to keep most cowboys in line. He walked the streets with his long hair flowing and his twin Colts at his side, a living symbol of law and order in a lawless land.

But Bill's time in Abilene ended tragically. In October 1871, he was involved in a shooting at the Alamo Saloon. When the smoke cleared, gambler Phil Coe was dead, but so was Bill's own deputy, Mike Williams, who had been accidentally shot by Bill in the confusion. This incident haunted Wild Bill for the rest of his life and marked the beginning of his decline as a lawman.

The technical aspects of Wild Bill's gunfighting skills were truly remarkable. He was ambidextrous and could shoot accurately with either hand. His preferred weapons were Navy Colt revolvers, which he kept in perfect condition and practiced with constantly. He understood that in a gunfight, speed was important, but accuracy was everything. A fast draw meant nothing if you couldn't hit your target.

Bill's shooting stance was also distinctive. Unlike many gunfighters who shot from the hip, Bill would bring his gun up to eye level and take careful aim, even in the heat of battle. This technique, combined with his natural ability and constant practice, made him one of the most accurate pistol shots of his era.

Wild Bill's fame spread far beyond the frontier through newspaper accounts and dime novels. Eastern writers were fascinated by this larger-than-life character who seemed to embody everything exciting and dangerous about the American West. Some of these accounts were exaggerated, but the core truth remained: Wild Bill Hickok was a real man who had done extraordinary things in extraordinary times.

In his later years, Bill tried his hand at show business, appearing in Buffalo Bill Cody's Wild West Show. However, he was never comfortable as a performer and preferred the real dangers of the frontier to the staged excitement of the show ring. He was a man of action, not an actor, and the artificial nature of show business didn't suit his temperament.

Wild Bill's end came in Deadwood, South Dakota, in 1876. He was playing poker in Nuttal & Mann's Saloon when Jack McCall, a drifter with a grudge, shot him in the back of the head. Bill died instantly, still holding his poker hand - aces and eights, which became known as the "dead man's hand." He was only 39 years old, but he had already lived several lifetimes worth of adventure.

The manner of Bill's death was particularly tragic because it violated everything he stood for. Throughout his life, he had faced his enemies head-on, giving them a fair chance in honest fights. To be shot in the back by a coward was a bitter irony for a man who had always fought with honor and courage.

Wild Bill Hickok's legacy extends far beyond his reputation as a gunfighter. He represented the best qualities of the American frontier: courage in the face of danger, a commitment to justice, and the willingness to stand up for what was right regardless of the personal cost. He showed that one man with skill, determination, and moral courage could make a difference in a lawless world.

His story also illustrates the importance of the Second Amendment and the right to keep and bear arms. Wild Bill's guns were not just tools of his trade - they were the instruments of justice in places where formal law enforcement was weak or nonexistent. He proved that in the hands of a good man, firearms could be a force for order and civilization rather than chaos and violence.

Wild Bill's influence on American culture has been enormous. He became the prototype for countless fictional gunfighters and lawmen, and his story has been told and retold in books, movies, and television shows. But behind all the legend and mythology was a real man who lived by a code of honor and who used his extraordinary skills to protect the innocent and uphold the law.

Today, Wild Bill Hickok is remembered as one of the greatest gunfighters in American history, but more importantly, he is remembered as a man who stood for justice and order in a time and place where both were in short supply. His story reminds us that the right to keep and bear arms is not just about individual protection, but about the broader responsibility that free people have to maintain law and order in their communities. In the hands of men like Wild Bill Hickok, firearms were instruments of civilization, tools that helped transform the wild frontier into a place where decent people could live and prosper in peace.

Here's a little-known fact that might surprise you: Calamity Jane and Wild Bill Hickok were not the romantic partners that legend suggests. Their brief acquaintance in Deadwood, South Dakota, created a famous but largely fictionalized story of a great romance. While Wild Bill never participated in any Wild West shows, Calamity Jane later performed in Buffalo Bill's Wild West Show, thrilling audiences with her riding and shooting skills.

Annie Oakley, "Little Sure Shot," became America's sweetheart and proved that firearms skills knew no gender boundaries. This remarkable woman could split a playing card edge-wise at 30 paces and hit a dime tossed in the air. She performed for royalty across Europe, including Kaiser Wilhelm II of Germany, and became a symbol of American excellence and precision.

Annie Oakley: America's Sharpshooter Sweetheart

Phoebe Ann Mosey was born in 1860 in a log cabin in rural Ohio, the daughter of poor farmers who struggled to make ends meet. She would grow up to become Annie Oakley, one of the most famous women in the world and a shining example of how American determination and skill could overcome any obstacle. Her story is not just about marksmanship - it's about the American dream, the power of hard work, and the way firearms skills could open doors that seemed permanently closed to a poor farm girl.

Annie's childhood was marked by hardship. Her father died when she was just six years old, leaving her mother to raise six children alone. The family was so poor that Annie was sent to live with another family, where she was essentially treated as an indentured servant. She endured terrible conditions and abuse before finally escaping back to her mother's home when she was about ten years old.

It was then that Annie discovered her extraordinary gift. Her family needed food, and Annie taught herself to shoot using her father's old rifle. She quickly discovered that she had an almost supernatural ability with firearms. She could hit targets that experienced hunters missed, and she could do it consistently, shot after shot. By the time she was twelve, Annie was providing most of the meat for her family's table through her hunting skills.

But Annie didn't just hunt for survival - she turned her shooting skills into a business. She began selling game to local hotels and restaurants, and her reputation for providing the finest, cleanest kills spread throughout the region. Hotel owners preferred Annie's game because her shots were so precise that the birds and animals were unmarked except for the single, perfectly placed bullet hole. This attention to detail and excellence would characterize everything Annie did throughout her life.

Annie's big break came in 1875 when she was just fifteen years old. A traveling marksman named Frank Butler came to Cincinnati and issued a challenge: he would pay $100 to anyone who could outshoot him. Local sportsmen arranged for Annie to take the challenge, though they didn't tell Frank that his opponent would be a teenage girl. The match was set for 25 shots at clay pigeons thrown from traps.

What happened next became the stuff of legend. Annie hit 23 out of 25 targets, while Frank Butler, an experienced professional marksman, hit only 22. Not only had this unknown farm girl defeated one of the best shooters in the country, but she had done it with grace and modesty that charmed everyone present, including Frank Butler himself. Frank was so impressed that he began courting Annie, and they were married a year later.

Frank Butler recognized that his wife's talent was extraordinary, and he became her manager and biggest supporter. In 1885, they joined Buffalo Bill's Wild West Show, where Annie would spend the next 17 years amazing audiences around the world. Buffalo Bill Cody himself gave her the stage name "Annie Oakley" and the nickname "Little Sure Shot."

Annie's performances were nothing short of miraculous. She could hit a dime tossed in the air, split a playing card edge-wise at 30 paces, and shoot the flame off a candle without melting the wax. She could hit six glass balls thrown in the air before any of them hit the ground, and she could do it while riding a galloping horse. One of her most famous tricks was shooting a cigarette from her husband's lips - a feat that required not just incredible accuracy but absolute trust between the couple.

But Annie's skills went far beyond trick shooting. She was a serious markswoman who understood the technical aspects of firearms and ballistics. She could shoot accurately with rifles, shotguns, and pistols. She was equally skilled with moving targets and stationary ones, and she could adapt to different lighting conditions and weather. Her consistency was perhaps her most remarkable trait - she rarely missed, even under pressure and in front of thousands of spectators.

Annie's fame spread around the world when Buffalo Bill's Wild West Show toured Europe in the 1880s and 1890s. She performed for Queen Victoria of England, who was so impressed that she requested a command performance. Annie also performed for Kaiser Wilhelm II of Germany, King Umberto I of Italy, and President Marie François Sadi Carnot of France. European royalty was fascinated by this American woman who could outshoot their best marksmen.

During one performance in Germany, Annie demonstrated her skills by shooting a cigarette from the lips of Crown Prince Wilhelm (later Kaiser Wilhelm II). This seemingly innocent demonstration would later take on historical significance when Wilhelm became Kaiser and led Germany into World War I. Some people jokingly suggested that if Annie's aim had been just slightly off that day, the course of world history might have been different.

Annie's success challenged conventional ideas about women's capabilities and helped pave the way for greater opportunities for women in America. She proved that skill and determination mattered more than gender, and she did it while maintaining her femininity and charm. She always performed in skirts and maintained impeccable manners, showing that a woman could be both an expert marksman and a lady.

Beyond her performing career, Annie was a passionate advocate for women's rights and firearms training. She believed that all women should learn to shoot, both for sport and for self-defense. She offered to train a regiment of women marksmen for the Spanish-American War, though the government declined her offer. She also taught thousands of women to shoot during her career, always emphasizing safety and proper technique.

Annie was also a strong supporter of hunting and conservation. She understood that hunters were the backbone of wildlife conservation efforts, and she used her fame to promote responsible hunting practices. She believed that hunting was not just about taking game, but about understanding and respecting nature.

Throughout her career, Annie maintained the highest standards of professionalism and sportsmanship. She never used her fame for personal gain at others' expense, and she was known for her generosity and kindness. She often performed at charity events and donated money to help orphans and other children in need.

Annie's technical skills were matched by her understanding of showmanship. She knew how to entertain an audience while demonstrating serious marksmanship skills. Her performances were carefully choreographed to build excitement and suspense, and she had an intuitive understanding of what would thrill spectators. She made shooting look effortless, but behind every performance were hours of practice and preparation.

One of Annie's most remarkable achievements was her longevity as a performer. She continued to amaze audiences well into her sixties, maintaining her accuracy and skill even as age began to take its toll. Her dedication to practice and her commitment to excellence never wavered, and she continued to set new records and achieve new feats throughout her career.

Annie's influence extended far beyond the world of shooting sports. She became a symbol of American excellence and ingenuity, proof that with hard work and determination, anyone could achieve greatness. Her story inspired countless young people, both male and female, to pursue their dreams regardless of the obstacles they faced.

The technical aspects of Annie's shooting were truly extraordinary. She used a variety of firearms throughout her career, but she was particularly known for her work with shotguns and rifles. She preferred lighter weapons that she could handle quickly and accurately, and she was constantly experimenting with different loads and techniques to improve her performance.

Annie's legacy lives on today in the millions of American women who participate in shooting sports. She proved that marksmanship is not about physical strength but about mental discipline, hand-eye coordination, and the ability to remain calm under pressure. These are qualities that anyone can develop with proper training and practice.

Perhaps most importantly, Annie Oakley demonstrated that the Second Amendment truly is for all Americans. She showed that the right to keep and bear arms is not limited by gender, background, or social status. Her success proved that in America, talent and hard work can overcome any obstacle, and that firearms skills can be a path to independence and success.

Annie Oakley died in 1926, but her legend lives on. She remains one of the most famous Americans of the 19th century, and her story continues to inspire new generations of shooters and dreamers. She proved that with a firearm in skilled hands, an American can achieve anything - even a poor farm girl from Ohio can become the most famous sharpshooter in the world.

The famous gunfight at the O.K. Corral in Tombstone wasn't just a random act of violence - it was a confrontation between lawmen and outlaws that lasted only about 30 seconds but became the stuff of legend. The Earp brothers, along with Doc Holliday, faced down the Clanton-McLaury gang in a showdown that epitomized the struggle between law and lawlessness on the frontier.

The Gunfight at the O.K. Corral: Thirty Seconds That Defined the West

October 26, 1881, dawned clear and cool in Tombstone, Arizona Territory. The silver mining boomtown was bustling with activity, but tension had been building for months between two factions that would soon face each other in the most famous gunfight in American history. What happened that afternoon would become the defining moment of the American frontier and a testament to the courage of lawmen who stood up for justice in a lawless land.

The story begins with the Earp brothers - Wyatt, Virgil, and Morgan - who had come to Tombstone seeking their fortune but found themselves serving as the town's law enforcement. Wyatt Earp was a veteran lawman who had served in Dodge City, Kansas, one of the toughest cow towns on the frontier. Virgil was the town marshal, and Morgan served as a deputy. These were men who understood that civilization required someone to stand between the innocent and those who would prey upon them.

Their ally was John Henry "Doc" Holliday, a dentist turned gambler and gunfighter who had befriended Wyatt Earp in Dodge City. Doc was dying of tuberculosis, but he was also one of the fastest and most accurate gunmen in the West. Despite his reputation as a dangerous man, Doc Holliday was fiercely loyal to his friends and had an unwavering sense of honor.

On the other side were the Clanton and McLaury brothers - Ike and Billy Clanton, and Tom and Frank McLaury. These men were part of a loose confederation of rustlers and outlaws who operated in the area around Tombstone. They represented the lawless element that plagued many frontier towns, men who believed that might made right and who had little respect for legal authority.

The tension had been building for months. The Earps suspected the Clantons and McLaurys of cattle rustling and stage robbery, while the cowboys resented the Earps' efforts to bring law and order to Tombstone. Personal animosities had developed, and threats had been made on both sides.

On the morning of October 26, Ike Clanton had been drinking heavily and making threats against the Earps. He had been armed and walking the streets of Tombstone, declaring his intention to kill the Earp brothers and Doc Holliday. Virgil Earp, as town marshal, arrested Ike for carrying weapons within the city limits - Tombstone had a gun ordinance that prohibited carrying firearms in town.

After being fined and released, Ike continued his threats. He was soon joined by his younger brother Billy, and the McLaury brothers, Tom and Frank. A fifth man, Billy Claiborne, was also with them. The group gathered near the O.K. Corral, armed and apparently preparing for a confrontation.

Citizens began reporting to the Earps that the cowboys were armed and making threats. Sheriff Johnny Behan, who was politically opposed to the Earps, attempted to disarm the group but was unsuccessful. The situation was rapidly spiraling out of control, and Virgil Earp realized that as town marshal, he had to act.

At approximately 3:00 PM, the three Earp brothers and Doc Holliday walked down Fremont Street toward the vacant lot near the O.K. Corral where the cowboys were gathered. Virgil carried a shotgun, Wyatt and Morgan had revolvers, and Doc Holliday carried both a revolver and a shotgun concealed under his long coat.

The Earps were not looking for a fight - they were attempting to enforce the law. Virgil called out to the cowboys to throw up their hands and surrender their weapons. What happened next is disputed, but witnesses agreed that someone shouted "Hold! I don't mean that!" and then the shooting began.

The gunfight lasted approximately thirty seconds, but in that brief time, more than thirty shots were fired. Billy Clanton and both McLaury brothers were killed. Virgil and Morgan Earp were wounded, and Doc Holliday received a slight wound. Wyatt Earp was the only participant who emerged unscathed. Ike Clanton and Billy Claiborne fled the scene without firing a shot.

The aftermath of the gunfight was almost as dramatic as the event itself. The Earps and Doc Holliday were arrested and charged with murder, but after a lengthy hearing, they were exonerated. The judge ruled that they had acted within their authority as law enforcement officers and that the shooting was justified.

However, the conflict was far from over. In December 1881, Virgil Earp was ambushed and severely wounded by unknown assailants. In March 1882, Morgan Earp was assassinated while playing billiards. Wyatt Earp responded by forming a federal posse and hunting down those he believed responsible for his brothers' attacks. This vendetta ride, as it came to be known, resulted in several more deaths and cemented Wyatt Earp's reputation as one of the most formidable lawmen of the frontier era.

The gunfight at the O.K. Corral became legendary for several reasons. First, it represented the classic confrontation between law and lawlessness that defined the American frontier. The Earps were not perfect men, but they were willing to risk their lives to uphold the law and protect their community. They understood that civilization required someone to stand up to those who would use violence and intimidation to get their way.

Second, the gunfight demonstrated the importance of marksmanship and firearms training. The Earps and Doc Holliday were skilled gunmen who had practiced their craft and understood the importance of accuracy under pressure. Their superior shooting skills and tactical awareness gave them the advantage in the confrontation.

Third, the gunfight showed the importance of courage and determination in the face of overwhelming odds. The Earps were outnumbered, but they did not back down from their duty. They understood that sometimes good men must be willing to fight to protect what is right.

The story of the O.K. Corral also illustrates the complex nature of frontier justice. The line between law and lawlessness was often blurred, and good men sometimes had to use violence to combat violence. The Earps were not saints, but they were on the side of law and order in a place where such concepts were often foreign.

The gunfight became the subject of countless books, movies, and television shows, making Wyatt Earp and Doc Holliday household names around the world. While Hollywood often took liberties with the facts, the basic story remained compelling: good men with guns standing up to bad men with guns, and justice prevailing in the end.

The legacy of the O.K. Corral extends far beyond that thirty-second gunfight in Tombstone. It represents the American ideal that ordinary citizens can and must be prepared to defend themselves and their communities against those who would do them harm. It shows that the right to keep and bear arms is not just about individual protection, but about the broader responsibility that free people have to maintain law and order in their society.

Today, as we face new challenges and new threats, the lesson of the O.K. Corral remains as relevant as ever. We must be prepared to stand up for what is right, even when it is dangerous to do so. We must understand that freedom is not free, and that sometimes good people must be willing to fight to preserve it. And we must never forget that the Second Amendment exists not just to protect our individual rights, but to ensure that we always have the means to defend our communities and our way of life against those who would destroy them.

What many people don't realize is that the Wild West was actually quite civilized in many ways. Towns like Dodge City, Tombstone, and Deadwood had newspapers, schools, churches, and thriving businesses. The presence of armed, law-abiding citizens actually helped maintain order and protect the innocent from those who would do them harm.

The Western movie genre captured the imagination of the world and spread the story of American courage and individualism to every corner of the globe. These films celebrated the values that made America great: the willingness to stand up for what's right, the importance of personal responsibility, and the idea that good people with guns can stop bad people with guns.

The legacy of the Wild West lives on today in the millions of Americans who embrace the shooting sports, who hunt to provide for their families, and who understand that the right to keep and bear arms is fundamental to maintaining a free society. The frontier may be gone, but the spirit of the Wild West - the spirit of freedom, self-reliance, and individual responsibility - remains alive and well in the American gun culture.

"On the far edge of civilization, where law rode on horseback and justice was drawn from the hip, legends were not written — they were lived."

Part 4:
The Modern Era
(1900-Present)

Chapter 11:
American Innovation and the Spirit of Enterprise

The early 20th century marked an extraordinary period of American innovation and industrial growth that would establish the United States as the world's leading manufacturing power. This era saw American firearms manufacturers reach new heights of excellence, producing weapons that were not only the finest in the world but also the most innovative and reliable ever created.

The period from 1900 to 1940 was truly the golden age of American firearms manufacturing. Companies like Colt, Winchester, Remington, and Smith & Wesson were producing firearms that were marvels of engineering and craftsmanship. The Winchester Model 1894, introduced in 1894 and continuing production well into this era, became one of the most successful sporting rifles in history. More than 7 million were produced, making it a favorite of hunters, ranchers, and sportsmen across America.

John Moses Browning, perhaps the greatest firearms inventor in history, revolutionized the industry during this period. His designs included the legendary Colt .45 automatic pistol, adopted by the U.S. military in 1911 and still in use today. Browning's genius lay not just in creating reliable weapons, but in designing firearms that could be mass-produced with precision and consistency. His automatic shotgun, the Browning Auto-5, remained in production for nearly a century - a testament to the brilliance of American engineering.

The Thompson submachine gun, developed by General John T. Thompson, showcased American innovation in response to the challenges of World War I. Though the war ended before it could be widely deployed, the "Tommy Gun" became an icon of American manufacturing prowess and would later serve Allied forces in World War II.

This era also saw the rise of American sporting culture around firearms. The National Rifle Association, founded in 1871, grew tremendously during this period, promoting marksmanship, hunting, and firearms safety. Shooting sports became increasingly popular, with Americans excelling in Olympic competition and establishing shooting as a respected recreational activity.

The period also witnessed the growth of hunting as both a conservation tool and a cherished American tradition. The Federal Aid in Wildlife Restoration Act of 1937, also known as the Pittman-Robertson Act, established a tax on firearms and ammunition that would fund wildlife conservation efforts. This brilliant piece of legislation, supported enthusiastically by hunters and gun owners, has generated billions of dollars for conservation and remains one of the most successful conservation funding mechanisms in history.

American firearms manufacturers during this era didn't just serve the domestic market - they became global leaders. American-made weapons were sought after worldwide for their quality, reliability, and innovation. This export success demonstrated American industrial superiority and helped establish the United States as a major player on the world stage.

The craftsmanship of this era was extraordinary. Firearms were not just functional tools but works of art, with intricate engraving, beautiful wood stocks, and precision machining that set the standard for the world. Companies took pride in their products and their workers, creating a culture of excellence that would define American manufacturing for generations.

Even when faced with challenges, American gun owners and manufacturers showed remarkable resilience and adaptability. They understood that their industry was not just about making products, but about preserving a fundamental American right and way of life. This period laid the foundation for the modern American firearms industry, which continues to lead the world in innovation, quality, and technological advancement.

The early 20th century proved that American ingenuity, combined with the freedom to innovate and compete, could produce results that amazed the world. The firearms industry of this era stands as a shining example of what American enterprise can accomplish when free people are allowed to pursue excellence.

The St. Valentine's Day Massacre: A Lesson in Law and Order

The 1920s brought unique challenges to American law enforcement, challenges that would test the resolve of both police officers and federal agents in ways never before experienced. The era of Prohibition created unprecedented criminal enterprises, and the St. Valentine's Day Massacre of 1929 became a defining moment that demonstrated both the dangers faced by law enforcement and the importance of ensuring that good people have the tools necessary to combat evil.

February 14, 1929, dawned cold and gray in Chicago, but it would become one of the most infamous days in American crime history. The events of that Valentine's Day morning would shock the nation and galvanize law enforcement agencies to take decisive action against organized crime.

The story begins with the complex criminal landscape of 1920s Chicago. Two major criminal organizations controlled different parts of the city's illegal activities. Al Capone, a shrewd businessman who happened to operate outside the law, controlled the South Side with an organization that generated enormous profits. On the North Side, George "Bugs" Moran led a rival organization that competed for the same territory and profits.

These criminal enterprises had access to military-grade weapons, including Thompson submachine guns that could fire 600 rounds per minute. While law-abiding citizens followed various regulations regarding firearms, criminals simply ignored all laws and obtained whatever weapons they needed through illegal channels. This created a dangerous imbalance where criminals were often better armed than the police officers trying to stop them.

By 1929, the rivalry between these organizations had escalated to unprecedented levels of violence. Both sides had survived multiple assassination attempts, and the situation was spiraling out of control. Something had to give, and unfortunately, it would be seven men who paid the ultimate price.

On the morning of February 14, four men - two dressed as police officers and two in civilian clothes - entered the S-M-C Cartage Company garage at 2122 North Clark Street, where seven members of Moran's organization were waiting for a shipment. The fake officers ordered the seven men to line up against the brick wall, as if conducting a routine arrest.

What happened next was swift and brutal. The assassins opened fire with Thompson submachine guns and shotguns, killing all seven men in a hail of bullets. The victims included some of Chicago's most notorious criminals, but they were also human beings who met a violent end in what became known as the St. Valentine's Day Massacre.

Ironically, Bugs Moran himself was not present that morning. Running late, he saw what he thought were police officers entering his headquarters and waited outside, unknowingly saving his own life while his associates were being killed inside.

When real police officers arrived at the scene, they found seven men dead or dying. Frank Gusenberg, despite being shot multiple times, was still alive when police arrived. When asked who had shot him, the mortally wounded man kept to the criminal code of silence, responding, "No one, nobody shot me." He died shortly afterward.

The St. Valentine's Day Massacre marked a turning point in the fight against organized crime. The brutality of the killings shocked the American public and galvanized federal law enforcement to take unprecedented action. This was when heroes like Eliot Ness and his team of federal agents, known as "The Untouchables," stepped forward to take on the criminal organizations that had terrorized American cities.

Ness and his agents represented the best of American law enforcement - incorruptible, dedicated, and willing to risk their lives to uphold the law. They understood that to combat criminals who had access to military-grade weapons, law enforcement needed to be equally well-armed and better trained. The Untouchables used the same Thompson submachine guns that the criminals used, but they used them in service of justice and the rule of law.

The federal response to organized crime demonstrated several important principles that remain relevant today. First, it showed that when criminals are heavily armed, law enforcement must have access to equally effective weapons. Second, it proved that dedicated, well-trained officers could overcome even the most powerful criminal organizations when they had the tools and support they needed.

The investigation and prosecution of Al Capone became a model for federal law enforcement. Unable to convict him for his violent crimes due to the code of silence among criminals, federal agents instead built a case against him for tax evasion. This innovative approach showed that American law enforcement could adapt and find new ways to bring criminals to justice.

The massacre also led to important developments in firearms regulation. The National Firearms Act of 1934 imposed registration requirements and taxes on certain types of weapons, including machine guns. While this law was intended to address the weapons used by organized crime, it was carefully crafted to respect the constitutional rights of law-abiding citizens while giving law enforcement additional tools to combat criminal organizations.

By the early 1930s, changes in policy had eliminated much of the economic incentive that had created these criminal enterprises in the first place. The end of Prohibition in 1933 removed the black market that had made organized crime so profitable, and without those enormous profits, the criminal organizations could no longer maintain their private armies or engage in the spectacular violence that had characterized the 1920s.

The St. Valentine's Day Massacre taught Americans several important lessons that remain relevant today. It showed that criminals will always find ways to obtain weapons, regardless of laws or regulations. It demonstrated that law enforcement needs adequate tools and training to combat well-armed criminals. And it proved that the best way to reduce criminal violence is often to address the underlying conditions that create criminal enterprises in the first place.

Perhaps most importantly, the massacre and its aftermath showed the resilience of American institutions and the rule of law. When faced with unprecedented criminal violence, American law enforcement adapted, innovated, and ultimately prevailed. Heroes like Eliot Ness proved that good people with guns, proper training, and unwavering dedication to justice could defeat even the most powerful criminal organizations.

The seven men who died in that Chicago garage were criminals, but their deaths served as a wake-up call that led to important improvements in American law enforcement. The massacre became a symbol of what happens when the balance of power shifts too far toward criminals, and it reinforced the importance of ensuring that law-abiding citizens and law enforcement officers have the means to defend themselves and their communities.

Today, as we face new challenges from organized crime, terrorism, and other threats, the lessons of the St. Valentine's Day Massacre remain as relevant as ever. We must ensure that our law enforcement officers have the training and equipment they need to protect our communities. We must remember that criminals will always find ways to obtain weapons, regardless of laws. And we must never forget that the Second Amendment exists not just to protect individual rights, but to ensure that good people always have the means to defend themselves against those who would do them harm.

The massacre was a dark chapter in American history, but it also demonstrated the strength and resilience of American institutions. It showed that when faced with unprecedented challenges, Americans can adapt, overcome, and emerge stronger than before. That spirit of resilience and determination continues to define American law enforcement and American gun culture to this day.

Chapter 12:
The Supreme Court Restores the Second Amendment

The story of the Supreme Court and the Second Amendment is ultimately a story of triumph - the triumph of constitutional principles over political expediency, the triumph of individual rights over government overreach, and the triumph of the Founding Fathers' vision over decades of judicial neglect. It is a story that shows how the American system of government, even when it strays from its founding principles, has the capacity to correct itself and return to the path of liberty.

For too long, the Second Amendment was treated as a second-class right by the courts. While other amendments in the Bill of Rights received robust protection, the Second Amendment was largely ignored or misinterpreted. But the American people never forgot what the Founding Fathers intended, and they never stopped fighting for their constitutional rights.

The turning point came with the landmark case of District of Columbia v. Heller in 2008. This case represented the culmination of decades of scholarship, advocacy, and legal strategy by dedicated defenders of the Second Amendment. The case involved Dick Heller, a security guard who wanted to keep a handgun in his home for protection but was prevented from doing so by Washington D.C.'s draconian gun ban.

Justice Antonin Scalia, writing for the majority, delivered one of the most important constitutional decisions in American history. The Court ruled definitively that the Second Amendment protects an individual right to keep and bear arms, unconnected to service in a militia. The decision vindicated what gun owners had always known - that the Second Amendment means what it says, and that the right to keep and bear arms is a fundamental individual right.

The Heller decision was a masterpiece of constitutional interpretation. Justice Scalia meticulously examined the text, history, and tradition of the Second Amendment, showing that the individual rights interpretation was not only correct but was the only interpretation consistent with the amendment's language and the Founding Fathers' intent. The decision demolished decades of flawed legal reasoning and restored the Second Amendment to its rightful place in the Constitution.

Two years later, the Court extended this victory in McDonald v. Chicago, ruling that the Second Amendment applies to state and local governments as well as the federal government. This decision ensured that Americans in every state would be protected by the Second Amendment, regardless of the political preferences of their local politicians.

The most recent triumph came in 2022 with New York State Rifle & Pistol Association v. Bruen, where the Court struck down New York's restrictive concealed carry law. Justice Clarence Thomas, writing for the majority, established that the Second Amendment protects the right to carry firearms in public for self-defense, and he created a new legal framework that will protect gun rights for generations to come.

These Supreme Court victories represent more than just legal wins - they represent the vindication of American principles and the restoration of constitutional government. They show that the American system works, that rights can be restored, and that the Constitution remains a living document that protects individual liberty.

The Court's journey on the Second Amendment also demonstrates the importance of appointing judges who understand and respect the Constitution. The justices who voted to protect Second Amendment rights understood that their job was not to make policy, but to interpret the law as written. They understood that the Constitution means what it says, and that the rights it protects are not subject to the whims of political fashion.

These decisions have had a profound impact on American law and society. They have struck down unconstitutional gun laws across the country, they have protected the rights of law-abiding gun owners, and they have sent a clear message that the Second Amendment is not a suggestion - it is the supreme law of the land.

The Supreme Court's restoration of the Second Amendment is a testament to the enduring wisdom of the Founding Fathers and the resilience of the American constitutional system. It shows that even when government strays from its proper role, the Constitution provides the tools necessary to restore liberty and protect individual rights.

Today, thanks to these landmark decisions, the Second Amendment stands stronger than ever. It is no longer a forgotten amendment or a second-class right. It is a fundamental constitutional guarantee that protects the right of all Americans to defend themselves, their families, and their freedom.

Chapter 13:
The Strength of American Gun Culture

American gun culture is one of the most vibrant, diverse, and positive aspects of American society. Far from being a source of division, it represents the best of American values: individual responsibility, self-reliance, respect for tradition, and a commitment to protecting family and community. This culture has produced some of the finest marksmen in the world, the most successful conservation programs in history, and a citizenry that understands the true meaning of freedom.

At the heart of American gun culture is the shooting sports community. From Olympic-level competition to weekend plinking, Americans have embraced firearms as tools of sport and recreation. The United States has dominated Olympic shooting sports for decades, producing champions like Kim Rhode, who has won six Olympic medals in shooting sports, and Vincent Hancock, a two-time Olympic gold medalist in skeet shooting. These athletes represent the pinnacle of American marksmanship and demonstrate the positive aspects of gun culture to the world.

The hunting community represents another cornerstone of American gun culture. America's 11 million hunters are the backbone of wildlife conservation in this country. Through hunting licenses, tags, and the excise taxes they pay on firearms and ammunition through the Pittman-Robertson Act, hunters contribute more than $1.6 billion annually to conservation efforts. This has resulted in one of the greatest conservation success stories in history - the recovery of species like white-tailed deer, wild turkey, and elk from near extinction to abundant populations.

The National Rifle Association, founded in 1871, has been instrumental in promoting firearms safety and education. The NRA's Eddie Eagle program has taught firearms safety to more than 32 million children, helping to reduce accidental firearms deaths to historic lows. The organization's instructor programs have trained hundreds of thousands of Americans in safe firearms handling, making the shooting sports one of the safest recreational activities in America.

American gun culture has also produced a thriving industry that employs hundreds of thousands of Americans and contributes billions to the economy. From major manufacturers like Smith & Wesson and Ruger to small custom gunmakers, the firearms industry represents American craftsmanship and innovation at its finest. These companies don't just make products - they preserve traditions, support communities, and maintain skills that have been passed down through generations.

The concealed carry movement represents one of the most significant developments in modern American gun culture. Starting with just a handful of states in the 1980s, the movement has grown to include all 50 states with some form of concealed carry law. This expansion has been accompanied by dramatic decreases in violent crime, demonstrating that an armed citizenry is indeed a polite citizenry.

Women represent the fastest-growing segment of American gun culture. Organizations like the Well Armed Woman and A Girl and a Gun have created supportive communities where women can learn firearms skills, practice shooting sports, and connect with like-minded individuals. Female participation in shooting sports has increased by more than 80% in recent years, showing that gun culture truly welcomes everyone.

The tactical and practical shooting communities have revolutionized firearms training and competition. Organizations like the International Practical Shooting Confederation (IPSC) and the United States Practical Shooting Association (USPSA) have created dynamic, challenging competitions that test real-world shooting skills. These sports have produced innovations in firearms, equipment, and training techniques that benefit everyone from law enforcement officers to civilian defenders.

American gun culture has also embraced technology and innovation. From advanced optics and ammunition to smart training systems and 3D printing, American gun owners are at the forefront of technological advancement. This spirit of innovation ensures that American firearms and accessories remain the best in the world.

Perhaps most importantly, American gun culture is fundamentally about values - the values that made America great. It's about taking responsibility for your own safety and the safety of your family. It's about respecting the rights of others while standing firm in defense of your own rights. It's about understanding that freedom requires vigilance and that the price of liberty is eternal vigilance.

The strength of American gun culture lies not in politics or controversy, but in the millions of law-abiding Americans who safely and responsibly exercise their Second Amendment rights every day. These are the people who teach their children to shoot, who volunteer at local gun clubs, who support conservation efforts, and who understand that the right to keep and bear arms is not just about guns - it's about freedom itself.

This culture has weathered every storm and emerged stronger. It has adapted to changing times while maintaining its core values. And it will continue to thrive because it represents something fundamental about the American character - the belief that free people have the right and responsibility to defend themselves, their families, and their country.

"American gun culture is not born of violence, but of virtue — responsibility, self-reliance, tradition, and the enduring duty to defend what we love."

Chapter 14: America Armed and Free - The Numbers Tell the Story

The statistics about gun ownership and defensive gun use in America tell a remarkable story - the story of a free people who have embraced their constitutional rights and used them to create one of the safest and most prosperous societies in human history. Far from being a source of problems, America's armed citizenry represents one of our nation's greatest strengths.

America is home to an estimated 393 million firearms in civilian hands - more than one gun for every person in the country. This represents the largest armed civilian population in world history, and it is a testament to American freedom and prosperity. Between 80 and 100 million Americans own firearms, making gun owners one of the largest demographic groups in the country. These are not extremists or radicals - they are teachers, doctors, farmers, business owners, and retirees who understand that the right to keep and bear arms is fundamental to American liberty.

The most common reason Americans own firearms is self-defense, and the numbers show that this is a wise choice. Defensive gun use occurs far more frequently than gun crimes, with estimates ranging from 500,000 to 2.5 million defensive gun uses annually. These are real people protecting themselves, their families, and their communities from criminals who would do them harm.

Consider these inspiring statistics: States with the highest rates of gun ownership tend to have the lowest rates of violent crime. The expansion of concealed carry laws has been accompanied by dramatic decreases in violent crime rates. Areas with the most restrictive gun laws often have the highest rates of gun violence, while areas that respect Second Amendment rights tend to be safer and more prosperous.

The hunting community alone contributes more than $80 billion annually to the American economy and supports more than 680,000 jobs. Through hunting licenses and excise taxes on firearms and ammunition, hunters contribute over $1.6 billion annually to wildlife conservation - making them the primary funders of conservation in America. This has resulted in one of the greatest conservation success stories in history, with species like white-tailed deer, wild turkey, and elk recovering from near extinction to abundant populations.

The firearms industry employs more than 340,000 Americans and contributes over $70 billion annually to the economy. These are high-paying, skilled manufacturing jobs that represent the best of American craftsmanship and innovation. American-made firearms are sought after worldwide for their quality, reliability, and precision.

Perhaps most importantly, the numbers show that America's gun owners are among the most law-abiding citizens in the country. Concealed carry permit holders are convicted of crimes at rates far lower than the general population - even lower than police officers. This demonstrates that gun ownership promotes responsibility and respect for the law.

The accident rate for firearms has declined dramatically over the past several decades, thanks to improved safety education and training programs. Organizations like the NRA have taught firearms safety to millions of Americans, making shooting sports one of the safest recreational activities in the country.

Perhaps most telling of all is the evidence about what happens when governments attempt to ban or severely restrict firearms. History shows us repeatedly that such bans only affect law-abiding citizens - criminals, by definition, don't follow laws. When guns are banned, law-abiding citizens turn in their firearms or refrain from purchasing them, while criminals continue to obtain guns through illegal channels.

We can see this pattern playing out in cities across America today. Chicago, with some of the strictest gun laws in the nation, consistently ranks among the most dangerous cities in America. Meanwhile, states like Vermont and New Hampshire, with minimal gun restrictions, have some of the lowest crime rates in the country. The pattern is clear: when good people are disarmed, bad people become bolder.

The same principle applies internationally. Countries that have banned firearms often see increases in other forms of violent crime. Criminals simply switch to different weapons - knives, clubs, acid attacks - while law-abiding citizens are left defenseless. In contrast, areas where citizens are armed and trained tend to have lower overall crime rates because criminals know they might face armed resistance.

This is why the Second Amendment is so crucial. It ensures that the balance of power remains with law-abiding citizens rather than shifting to criminals and tyrants. When criminals know that their potential victims might be armed, they think twice before committing crimes. When governments know that their citizens are armed, they think twice before becoming tyrannical.

The evidence is overwhelming: gun bans don't reduce crime - they simply ensure that only criminals have guns. The Second Amendment, by contrast, ensures that good people have the means to defend themselves against those who would do them harm.

These numbers tell the real story of guns in America - not a story of violence and fear, but a story of freedom, responsibility, and the positive impact of an armed citizenry on society. They show that the Founding Fathers were right to trust the American people with the right to keep and bear arms, and they demonstrate that this trust has been well-placed.

"The right to bear arms is not a license for lawlessness; it is the surest safeguard of peace, for it empowers the just and deters the wicked."

Chapter 15:
The American Way - Guns as Part of Our Heritage

The role of firearms in American culture goes far beyond politics or controversy - it represents something fundamental about who we are as a people. From the earliest colonial settlements to the modern day, firearms have been woven into the fabric of American life, representing our values of self-reliance, individual responsibility, and the pioneering spirit that built this great nation.

Hunting represents one of the oldest and most cherished American traditions. For millions of Americans, hunting is not just a recreational activity - it's a way of connecting with nature, providing for their families, and passing down traditions from generation to generation. The American hunter is a conservationist, a provider, and a steward of the land. Hunting teaches patience, discipline, respect for wildlife, and an understanding of our place in the natural world.

The tradition of fathers and mothers teaching their children to shoot is as American as apple pie. These moments around the shooting bench or in the hunting blind create bonds that last a lifetime and pass down values that have made America strong. Children learn safety, responsibility, respect for firearms, and the importance of following rules. They learn that with rights come responsibilities, and that freedom requires discipline.

Sport shooting has become one of America's fastest-growing recreational activities. From trap and skeet to practical shooting competitions, Americans have embraced firearms as tools of sport and recreation. These activities promote excellence, precision, and friendly competition. They bring together people from all walks of life who share a common interest in marksmanship and the shooting sports.

The collecting of firearms represents another important aspect of American gun culture. Collectors preserve history, maintain craftsmanship traditions, and appreciate the artistry that goes into creating fine firearms. Whether it's a Civil War musket, a classic Winchester lever-action, or a modern precision rifle, each firearm tells a story about American innovation, craftsmanship, and heritage.

The portrayal of firearms in American entertainment has helped spread American values around the world. From the classic Western films that showed the importance of standing up for what's right, to modern action movies that celebrate the hero who protects the innocent, American entertainment has consistently portrayed firearms as tools in the hands of good people fighting against evil. These stories resonate because they reflect fundamental American values about justice, courage, and the responsibility to protect those who cannot protect themselves.

The growth of women's participation in shooting sports represents one of the most positive developments in modern American gun culture. Women are the fastest-growing segment of new gun owners, and they're embracing everything from competitive shooting to hunting to personal protection. Organizations like the Well Armed Woman and A Girl and a Gun have created supportive communities where women can learn, compete, and excel in the shooting sports.

The tactical and practical shooting communities have revolutionized firearms training and brought military and law enforcement techniques to civilian shooters. These disciplines emphasize real-world skills, quick decision-making, and the ability to perform under pressure. They've produced innovations in equipment, training methods, and safety protocols that benefit everyone from competitive shooters to law enforcement officers.

American gun culture has also embraced technology and innovation in ways that continue to amaze the world. From advanced optics and precision ammunition to smart training systems and cutting-edge manufacturing techniques, American gun owners and manufacturers remain at the forefront of technological advancement. This spirit of innovation ensures that American firearms and accessories remain the best in the world.

Perhaps most importantly, American gun culture is fundamentally optimistic and forward-looking. It's about building a better future for our children and grandchildren. It's about maintaining the skills and traditions that have served us well for more than two centuries. It's about understanding that freedom is not free, and that each generation must be prepared to defend the liberties that previous generations have passed down to us.

The Simple Truth About Firearms

In all the debates about gun rights and gun control, one fundamental truth often gets lost: a gun cannot point itself and pull its own trigger. This simple statement cuts through all the political rhetoric and gets to the heart of the matter. Firearms are inanimate objects - pieces of metal, wood, and polymer that have no will, no intent, and no ability to act on their own.

A gun sitting on a table will remain there forever unless a human being picks it up. It cannot load itself, aim itself, or fire itself. It requires human hands to operate it, human eyes to aim it, and human decision-making to use it. The gun is merely a tool, no different from a hammer, a knife, or an automobile - all of which can be used for good or evil depending on the person wielding them.

This truth is so obvious that it seems almost silly to state it, yet it's often forgotten in discussions about firearms. When we hear about gun violence, we're really hearing about people violence - individuals who have made the conscious decision to use a tool to harm others. The millions of firearms owned by law-abiding Americans never hurt anyone because their owners never choose to use them for evil purposes.

Every day in America, millions of firearms remain safely stored in homes, gun safes, and holsters without harming a single person. They sit quietly, waiting to be used for legitimate purposes: hunting, sport shooting, collecting, or protection. They pose no threat to anyone because they cannot act without human intervention.

The vast majority of American gun owners understand this responsibility completely. They know that owning a firearm means accepting the responsibility to use it safely, legally, and ethically. They teach their children gun safety, they practice regularly to maintain their skills, and they store their firearms securely. They understand that with the right to keep and bear arms comes the responsibility to exercise that right wisely.

This is why focusing on the tool rather than the person using it misses the point entirely. A person intent on causing harm will find a way to do so, regardless of the tools available. History is filled with examples of violence committed with knives, clubs, vehicles, explosives, and countless other implements. The common factor is not the tool - it's the human decision to cause harm.

Conversely, when good people have access to firearms, they use them to protect themselves and others. Every year, Americans use firearms millions of times to stop crimes, protect their families, and preserve their lives. In these cases, the same tool that could be used for evil is instead used for good - because it's in the hands of good people making good decisions.

The American gun owner understands this fundamental truth: firearms don't make people violent any more than cameras make people photographers. It's the person behind the tool who determines how it's used. This is why American gun culture emphasizes training, responsibility, and ethical behavior. It's why we teach our children to respect firearms, to understand their power, and to use them only for legitimate purposes.

The simple truth that a gun cannot point and pull its own trigger should guide all discussions about firearms policy. Laws that focus on restricting the tools while ignoring the behavior of the people using them are fundamentally misguided. Real solutions to violence must address the human factors - mental health, criminal behavior, and moral education - rather than trying to control inanimate objects.

The American way with firearms is fundamentally optimistic and forward-looking. It's about building a better future for our children and grandchildren. It's about maintaining the skills and traditions that have served us well for more than two centuries. It's about understanding that freedom is not free, and that each generation must be prepared to defend the liberties that previous generations have passed down to us.

The American way with firearms is not about conflict or division - it's about unity around shared values. It's about understanding that the right to keep and bear arms is not just about guns, but about the fundamental principle that free people have the right and responsibility to defend themselves, their families, and their country. This is what makes America unique, and this is what will keep America free for generations to come.

"A gun cannot act on its own — it is the hand and the heart behind it that decide its purpose."

Chapter 16:
The Future of Freedom - The Second Amendment in the 21st Century

The future of the Second Amendment has never been brighter. Thanks to landmark Supreme Court decisions, growing public support for gun rights, and a new generation of Americans who understand the importance of constitutional freedoms, the right to keep and bear arms is more secure today than it has been in decades. The Second Amendment is not just surviving in the 21st century - it is thriving.

The Supreme Court's decisions in Heller, McDonald, and Bruen have fundamentally transformed the legal landscape for gun rights. These decisions have established that the Second Amendment protects an individual right to keep and bear arms, that this right applies to all levels of government, and that any restrictions on this right must meet the highest constitutional standards. The Court has created a legal framework that will protect gun rights for generations to come.

The expansion of concealed carry rights across America represents one of the most significant victories for constitutional rights in modern history. From just a handful of states with concealed carry laws in the 1980s, we now have all 50 states with some form of concealed carry recognition. This expansion has been accompanied by dramatic decreases in violent crime, proving that an armed citizenry is indeed a safer citizenry.

Constitutional carry - the right to carry a firearm without a government permit - is spreading rapidly across America. More than half the states now recognize constitutional carry, and this number continues to grow each year. This represents a return to the original understanding of the Second Amendment, where the right to keep and bear arms was understood to be a natural right that required no government permission.

The next generation of Americans is embracing gun rights like never before. Young people are flocking to shooting sports, women are the fastest-growing segment of new gun owners, and minorities are increasingly recognizing that the Second Amendment protects everyone's right to self-defense. The future of gun rights is diverse, inclusive, and growing stronger every day.

Technological innovation continues to advance the cause of gun rights. From 3D printing that makes it impossible to ban firearms, to smart training systems that make firearms education more accessible, to advanced manufacturing techniques that make firearms more reliable and affordable, technology is ensuring that the right to keep and bear arms will remain viable and relevant in the digital age.

The firearms industry continues to innovate and grow, creating jobs, supporting communities, and producing the finest firearms in the world. American gun manufacturers are not just surviving in the global marketplace - they are dominating it. American-made firearms are sought after worldwide for their quality, reliability, and innovation.

The legal challenges to unconstitutional gun laws are succeeding at an unprecedented rate. Courts across the country are striking down magazine bans, assault weapon bans, and other restrictions that violate the Second Amendment. The legal momentum is clearly on the side of gun rights, and this trend will only accelerate in the coming years.

The political landscape is also shifting in favor of gun rights. More Americans than ever before support the right to keep and bear arms, and politicians who oppose gun rights are finding themselves on the wrong side of public opinion. The Second Amendment has become a winning political issue, and candidates who support gun rights are winning elections across the country.

Perhaps most importantly, the American people are rediscovering the fundamental importance of the Second Amendment. Recent events have reminded Americans that the police cannot be everywhere, that government cannot protect everyone, and that ultimately, each person is responsible for their own safety and the safety of their family. This realization is driving millions of Americans to exercise their Second Amendment rights for the first time.

The future will bring new challenges, of course. There will always be those who seek to restrict our rights, who believe that government knows better than the people, and who fear the freedom that the Second Amendment represents. But these challenges will be met by a generation of Americans who understand that freedom is not free, and who are willing to fight to preserve the rights that previous generations have passed down to us.

CHAPTER 16: THE FUTURE OF FREEDOM - THE SECOND AMENDMENT IN THE 21ST CENTURY

The Second Amendment is not just a relic of the past - it is a living, breathing guarantee of freedom that is more relevant today than ever before. In an uncertain world, it provides the ultimate insurance policy against tyranny. In a dangerous world, it provides the means for good people to protect themselves and their loved ones. In a free world, it represents the fundamental principle that the people, not the government, are sovereign.

The future of the Second Amendment is the future of freedom itself. And that future has never looked brighter.

107

Conclusion: The Eternal Flame of Freedom

As we reach the end of our journey through the history of the Second Amendment, we can see clearly that this remarkable constitutional provision is far more than just words on parchment. It is the embodiment of the American spirit, the guardian of our freedoms, and the eternal flame that has kept the light of liberty burning bright for more than two centuries.

From the English Bill of Rights to the colonial militias, from the Declaration of Independence to the Constitutional Convention, from the frontier settlements to the modern suburbs, the story of the Second Amendment is the story of America itself. It is the story of a people who refused to be subjects, who demanded to be citizens, and who understood that freedom requires both vigilance and the means to defend it.

The Founding Fathers, in their infinite wisdom, understood something that many modern politicians seem to have forgotten: that the right to keep and bear arms is not about hunting, though it protects that noble tradition. It is not about sport shooting, though it safeguards that enjoyable pastime. It is not even primarily about self-defense, though it guarantees that fundamental right. At its core, the Second Amendment is about power - the power of the people to remain free.

Today, as we face uncertain times and new challenges, the Second Amendment remains as relevant as ever. In a world where evil still exists, where criminals still prey on the innocent, and where governments still have the capacity for tyranny, the right to keep and bear arms stands as the ultimate guarantee that the American people will remain free.

The millions of Americans who exercise their Second Amendment rights every day are the true guardians of freedom. They are the hunters who teach their children respect for nature and responsibility for their actions. They are the competitive shooters who pursue excellence and precision. They are the collectors who preserve history and craftsmanship. They are the defenders who stand ready to protect their families and communities. And they are the citizens who understand that freedom is not free.

The Second Amendment has survived every challenge, weathered every storm, and emerged stronger than ever. It has protected us from foreign enemies and domestic tyrants. It has enabled us to build the greatest civilization in human history. And it will continue to guard our freedoms for generations to come.

As we look to the future, we can be confident that the Second Amendment will continue to evolve and adapt to new circumstances while maintaining its essential purpose. New technologies will emerge, new challenges will arise, and new generations will take up the responsibility of defending freedom. But the fundamental principle will remain unchanged: that free people have the right and responsibility to defend themselves, their families, and their country.

The story of Sarah McKinley, with which we began this book, is the story of the Second Amendment in action. It is the story of an ordinary American who, when faced with extraordinary circumstances, had the means to protect herself and her child. It is the story of freedom working exactly as the Founding Fathers intended.

The Second Amendment is not just our inheritance from the past - it is our gift to the future. It is our promise to our children and grandchildren that they will live in a free country, where the government serves the people and not the other way around. It is our commitment to the principle that has made America the beacon of hope for the world: that all people are created equal and endowed by their Creator with certain unalienable rights.

The right to keep and bear arms shall not be infringed. These eight words have protected American freedom for more than two centuries, and they will continue to do so for centuries to come. They are our shield against tyranny, our guarantee of liberty, and our eternal flame of freedom.

May that flame burn bright forever, and may future generations of Americans understand, as we do, that the Second Amendment is not just about guns - it is about freedom itself. And freedom, once lost, is not easily regained.

The Second Amendment: A right for all Americans, a guardian of freedom, and a promise to the future that liberty will endure.

"A well regulated Militia, being necessary to the security of a free State, the right of the people to keep and bear Arms, shall not be infringed."
- **The Second Amendment to the United States Constitution
Ratified December 15, 1791**

Appendix A: Key Constitutional Texts

The Second Amendment to the United States Constitution

A well regulated Militia, being necessary to the security of a free State, the right of the people to keep and bear Arms, shall not be infringed.

The Third Amendment to the United States Constitution

No Soldier shall, in time of peace be quartered in any house, without the consent of the Owner, nor in time of war, but in a manner to be prescribed by law.

The Sixth Amendment to the United States Constitution

In all criminal prosecutions, the accused shall enjoy the right to a speedy and public trial, by an impartial jury of the State and district wherein the crime shall have been committed, which district shall have been previously ascertained by law, and to be informed of the nature and cause of the accusation; to be confronted with the witnesses against him; to have compulsory process for obtaining witnesses in his favor, and to have the Assistance of Counsel for his defence.

The Tenth Amendment to the United States Constitution

The powers not delegated to the United States by the Constitution, nor prohibited by it to the States, are reserved to the States respectively, or to the people.

Appendix B: Key Historical Documents

The English Bill of Rights (1689) - Excerpt

That the subjects which are Protestants may have arms for their defence suitable to their conditions and as allowed by law.

The Virginia Declaration of Rights (1776) - Excerpt

That a well regulated militia, composed of the body of the people, trained to arms, is the proper, natural, and safe defense of a free state; that standing armies, in time of peace, should be avoided as dangerous to liberty; and that in all cases the military should be under strict subordination to, and governed by, the civil power.

The Declaration of Independence (1776) - Excerpt

We hold these truths to be self-evident, that all men are created equal, that they are endowed by their Creator with certain unalienable Rights, that among these are Life, Liberty and the pursuit of Happiness.--That to secure these rights, Governments are instituted among Men, deriving their just powers from the consent of the governed, --That whenever any Form of Government becomes destructive of these ends, it is the Right of the People to alter or to abolish it, and to institute new Government, laying its foundation on such principles and organizing its powers in such form, as to them shall seem most likely to effect their Safety and Happiness.

Appendix C: Firearms of the Civil War

Springfield Model 1861 - Type: Rifle-Musket - Caliber: .58
Notes: The most widely used infantry weapon of the Union Army.
Spencer Repeating Rifle - Type: Repeating Rifle - Caliber: .52
Notes: Lever-action rifle that gave Union cavalry a significant firepower advantage.
Henry Rifle - Type: Repeating Rifle - Caliber: .44
Notes: Famous for its high rate of fire, known as "the gun you could load on Sunday and shoot all week."
Colt Army Model 1860 - Type: Revolver - Caliber: .44
Notes: The standard sidearm for the Union cavalry.
Gatling Gun - Type: Hand-cranked Machine Gun - Caliber: .58
Notes: One of the first successful machine guns, used in limited numbers.
Richmond Rifle-Musket - Type: Rifle-Musket - Caliber: .58
Notes: The primary infantry weapon of the Confederacy, based on the Springfield design.
LeMat Revolver - Type: Revolver - Caliber: .42/.63
Notes: Unique Confederate revolver with a secondary shotgun barrel.
Whitworth Rifle - Type: Sniper Rifle - Caliber: .451
Notes: A highly accurate British-made rifle used by Confederate sharpshooters.
Parrott Rifle - Type: Artillery - Caliber: Various
Notes: A common type of rifled cannon used by both sides.
12-pounder Napoleon - Type: Artillery - Caliber: 4.62 inches
Notes: The most popular smoothbore cannon of the war, used by both sides.

Timeline of the Second Amendment

1689: The English Bill of Rights is passed, protecting the right of Protestants to bear arms.

1775: The American Revolution begins with the Battles of Lexington and Concord.

1787: The Constitutional Convention is held in Philadelphia.

1791: The Bill of Rights, including the Second Amendment, is ratified.

1794: The Whiskey Rebellion is suppressed by the federal government.

1865: The Civil War ends, and the Thirteenth Amendment is ratified, abolishing slavery.

1866: The Civil Rights Act is passed, protecting the right of all citizens to bear arms.

1871: The National Rifle Association is founded.

1876: The Supreme Court rules in United States v. Cruikshank that the Second Amendment does not apply to the states.

1911: The Sullivan Act is passed in New York, requiring a license to possess a handgun.

1934: The National Firearms Act is passed, regulating machine guns and other weapons.

1939: The Supreme Court rules in United States v. Miller that the Second Amendment protects the right to bear arms only in connection with militia service.

1968: The Gun Control Act is passed, expanding federal regulation of firearms.

1993: The Brady Handgun Violence Prevention Act is passed, mandating background checks for handgun purchases.

2008: The Supreme Court rules in District of Columbia v. Heller that the Second Amendment protects an individual's right to possess a firearm for self-defense.

2010: The Supreme Court rules in McDonald v. Chicago that the Second Amendment applies to the states.

2022: The Supreme Court rules in New York State Rifle & Pistol Association v. Bruen that the Second Amendment protects the right to carry a firearm in public for self-defense.

[4] District of Columbia v. Heller, 554 U.S. 570 (2008).

SOURCES

Historical Documents

English Bill of Rights (1689). The Avalon Project, Yale Law School. Accessed September 8, 2025. https://avalon.law.yale.edu/17th_century/england.asp

The Declaration of Independence (1776). National Archives. https://www.archives.gov/founding-docs/declaration-transcript

The Constitution of the United States (1787). National Archives. https://www.archives.gov/founding-docs/constitution-transcript

News and Media

Sarah McKinley Case (2011). Multiple news sources reported on the Oklahoma home defense incident, including local and national media coverage of the 911 call and subsequent legal proceedings.

Historical Records

Historical information about Hannah Duston, Nancy Hart, Daniel Boone, and other colonial and Revolutionary War figures is drawn from established historical records, contemporary accounts, and public historical archives.

Information about Civil War firearms and military history is based on documented military records, manufacturer specifications, and historical accounts from the period.

Note: This book presents well-established historical facts, events, and figures that are part of the public historical record. Specific dates, battles, and biographical information are drawn from multiple historical sources and archives.

INDEX

A
Abenaki, 10, 11
Adams, John, See entries under Founding Fathers
Adams, Samuel, See entries under Founding Fathers
American frontier, 9, 11, 13, 16, 69, 73, 78, 80
American Revolution, 1, 43, 111
    Declaration of Independence and, 21-23
    Nancy Hart's role in, 23-26
    See also Revolutionary War

B
Benjamin, Franklin, 34
Berdan Sharpshooters, 59
Bill of Rights, 7, 8, 32, 37-40, 42, 47, 91, 109, 111
    English Bill of Rights (1689), 7, 8, 109, 111
    First Amendment, See First Amendment
    Second Amendment, See Second Amendment
    Third Amendment, 22
    Sixth Amendment, 22
Billings, John, 56
Boone, Daniel, 16, 17, 19, 20
    siege of Boonesborough, 16-20
Boonesborough, 16-20
    siege of, 19
Boston, 11, 15
Boston Massacre, 15
British Crown, 15, 22, 38
Broad River, 23
Burton, James, 58

C
California Joe Milner, See Milner, California Joe
Civil War, 44, 55, 57, 59-61, 63, 64, 68-70, 101, 111, 112
    Confederate firearms, 57-58
    Union firearms, 55-56
    innovation and industry during, 55-60
Colonial America, 1, 12
    frontier life, 9-13
    gun laws, 7-8
    militia system, 7-9
Colt, Samuel, 57
Concord, Battle of, 15, 111
Confederacy, 57, 58
    firearms manufacturing, 57-58
    See also Civil War
Confederate Army, 59
Consent of the governed, 21, 22
Constitution, U.S., 7, 13, 22, 30, 32, 33, 35-42, 45, 47, 91, 92, 110
    Bill of Rights, See Bill of Rights
    Constitutional Convention, 1, 29-35, 37, 39, 109, 111
    Second Amendment, See Second Amendment
Constitutional Convention, 1, 29-35, 37, 39, 109, 111
Continental Army, 23, 29
Cotton Mather, 12

D
Declaration of Independence, 21-23, 25, 35, 109
    right of revolution and, 21-22
    Thomas Jefferson and, 21
Duston, Hannah, 9, 10, 12, 13
    captivity and escape, 10-12
Duston, Thomas, 10

E
English Bill of Rights (1689), 7, 8, 109, 111

F
Firearms
    12-gauge shotgun, 3
    12-pounder Napoleon, 59
    Colt Army Model 1860, 57
    flintlock musket, 1
    Gatling gun, 58
    Griswold & Gunnison, 58
    Henry rifle, 56, 60
    hunting knife, 3
    Kentucky rifle, See Kentucky rifle
    LeMat revolvers, 58
    Minié ball, 55
    musket, 1, 9, 24, 55, 57, 101
    Napoleon cannon, 59
    Parrott rifle, 58
    pistol, 3, 23, 70, 72, 85, 92, 111
    Richmond rifle-musket, 57
    rifle-musket, 55, 57
    rifling, 19, 55
    shotgun, 3, 58, 79, 85
    Spencer repeating rifle, 56
    Springfield Model 1861, 55
    tomahawk, 11
    Whitworth rifle, 58
First District of Columbia Cavalry, 57
Flintlock musket, 1

INDEX

F (continued)

Founding Fathers, 12, 13, 29, 33-36, 49, 52, 59, 63, 91, 92, 109, 110
   Adams, John, See Adams, John
   Adams, Samuel, See Adams, Samuel
   Franklin, Benjamin, 34
   Hamilton, Alexander, 31, 49
   Henry, Patrick, 31, 32, 37
   Jefferson, Thomas, 21
   Madison, James, 30, 39
   Mason, George, 31, 39
   Sherman, Roger, 33
   Washington, George, 29, 47
Franklin, Benjamin, 34
Freedom, 1, 3, 11-13, 20, 21, 23, 26, 29, 34-36, 41, 44, 45, 47-49, 51, 52, 60, 61, 63, 64, 68, 70, 81, 86, 92, 93, 95, 97, 99, 101, 102, 104-107, 109, 110
   right to bear arms and, 1-3, 7-8, 15-16
   tyranny and, See Tyranny

G

Gatling, Dr. Richard, 58
Gatling gun, 58
George III, King, See King George III
Georgia, 23, 25, 40, 56, 58
   backcountry, 23, 25
   Nancy Hart and, 23-26
Glorious Revolution (1688), 7
Griswold & Gunnison, 58

H

Hamilton, Alexander, 31, 49
Harpers Ferry, 57, 58
Hart, Benjamin, 23
Hart, Nancy, 23, 25, 26
   Revolutionary War exploits, 23-26
   War Woman of Georgia, 23-26
Hart, Nancy Morgan, See Hart, Nancy
Hartford, 57
Haverhill, Massachusetts, 10
Henry, Patrick, 31, 32, 37
Henry rifle, 56, 60

I

Interchangeable parts, 56

J

James II, King, 7
Jefferson, Thomas, 21
   Declaration of Independence and, 21

K

Kentucky, 16-20
   Boonesborough, 16-20
Kentucky rifle, 19, 55
King George III, 22
King James II, 7
King Philip, 9
   See also Metacomet
King Philip's War, 9
King William's War, 10

L

Lafayette, Marquis de, 34, 44
Lee, General Robert E., 58
LeMat, Dr. Jean Alexandre, 58
LeMat revolvers, 58
Leonardson, Samuel, 11
Lexington, Battle of, 1, 3, 15, 111
Lexington Green, 3
Liberty, 1-3, 7, 15, 21, 23, 25, 26, 29-42, 44, 45, 47, 48, 63, 91, 92, 95, 97, 109, 110, 112
   Declaration of Independence and, 21-23
   right to bear arms and, 1-3, 7-8
Lincoln, President Abraham, 56
Loyalists, 23, 24
   Nancy Hart and, 23-24

M

Madison, James, 30, 39
Manufacturing
   interchangeable parts, 56
   precision manufacturing, 55, 57, 60
   See also Springfield Armory; Richmond Armory
Marquis de Lafayette, 34, 44
Martin, Justin, 3
Mason, George, 31, 39
Massachusetts, 10, 11, 13, 40, 42, 56
   Boston, 11, 15
   Haverhill, 10
   Lexington, 1, 3, 15, 111
   Worcester, 11
Massachusetts General Assembly, 11
Mather, Cotton, 12
McKinley, Sarah, 2, 3, 110
   self-defense case, 2-3
Merrimack River, 11
Metacomet, 9
   See also King Philip

INDEX

M (continued)
Militia, 7-9, 15, 31-34, 38-41, 43, 48, 52, 91, 110, 111
   colonial militia system, 7-9
   well-regulated militia, 8, 32, 39
Minié ball, 55
Musket, 1, 9, 24, 55, 57, 101
   flintlock musket, 1
   rifle-musket, 55, 57
   smoothbore musket, See musket

N
Nancy Hart, See Hart, Nancy
Napoleon cannon, 59
Natural rights, 32, 35, 43
Neff, Mary, 10
New England, 9
   King Philip's War, 9
North Carolina, 23

O
Oklahoma, 2
   Sarah McKinley case, 2-3

P
Parrott, Robert Parker, 58
Parrott rifle, 58
Patriots, 15, 23
   Nancy Hart and, 23-26
Pennsylvania rifle, See Kentucky rifle
Philadelphia, 29, 30, 47, 111
   Constitutional Convention, 29-35
Philip, King, See King Philip
Pistol, 3, 23, 70, 72, 85, 92, 111
Powell, Ben, 58
Precision manufacturing, 55, 57, 60

R
Remington, 55, 60, 85
Revere, Paul, 15
Revolutionary War, 15, 16, 23, 25, 29, 47, 112
   Daniel Boone and, 16-20
   Hannah Duston and, 9-13
   Nancy Hart and, 23-26
   See also American Revolution
Richmond Armory, 57
Richmond rifle-musket, 57
Rifle-musket, 55, 57
Rifling, 19, 55
Right of revolution, 21
   Declaration of Independence and, 21-22

R (continued)
Right to bear arms, 8, 15, 16, 30, 32, 34-36, 38, 42-44, 99, 111, 112
   English inheritance, 7-8
   frontier necessity, 9-13
   See also Second Amendment
Right to keep and bear arms, See Right to bear arms; Second Amendment

S
Second Amendment, 1-3, 7-10, 12, 16, 18-24, 26, 29, 30, 32-45, 47-50, 52, 56, 58, 60, 61, 64, 66, 68, 70, 72-74, 76, 78, 80, 81, 86, 88-92, 94, 95, 97-99, 102, 104-107, 109-112
   colonial foundations, 7-13
   Constitutional Convention and, 29-35
   Declaration of Independence and, 21-23
   English inheritance, 7-8
   frontier necessity, 9-13
   militia and, 31-34, 38-41
   natural rights and, 32, 35, 43
   self-defense and, 2-3, 9-13, 35, 38, 41
   tyranny and, 7-8, 15-16, 21-23
Sedgwick, General John, 58
Self-defense, 9, 11, 12, 35, 38, 41, 52, 63, 68, 76, 92, 97, 105, 109, 111
   frontier necessity, 9-13
   Hannah Duston, 9-13
   Nancy Hart, 23-26
   Sarah McKinley, 2-3
Shenandoah Valley, 57
Sheridan, General Philip, 57
Sherman, Roger, 33
Shotgun, 3, 58, 79, 85
   12-gauge shotgun, 3
Sixth Amendment, 22
Spencer, Christopher, 56
Spencer repeating rifle, 56
Spotsylvania, Battle of, 58
Springfield Armory, 55, 56, 60
Springfield Model 1861, 55
Standing army, 7, 30, 40, 42
   colonial distrust of, 7-8
   militia as alternative, 7-9
Stuart, General J.E.B., 58

INDEX

T
Tenth Massachusetts Battery, 56
Third Amendment, 22
Thomas Jefferson, See Jefferson, Thomas
Tomahawk, 11
Tyranny, 7, 8, 15, 16, 22, 23, 26, 29-31, 33-35, 37, 38, 42, 64, 107, 109, 110
  Declaration of Independence and, 21-23
  right to resist, 21-22, 29-35
  Second Amendment and, 7-8, 15-16, 21-23

U
Unalienable rights, 21, 110
  Declaration of Independence and, 21
Union Army, 55, 70
  firearms, 55-56
  See also Civil War

V
Virginia, 31, 32, 37, 39, 42, 43, 56

W
Wampanoag, 9
  King Philip's War, 9
Washington, George, 29, 47
Well-regulated militia, 8, 32, 39
  See also Militia
Whitworth rifle, 58
Wild West, 1, 69, 71-73, 75, 77, 79, 81
Winchester, 55, 60, 85, 101
Worcester, Massachusetts, 11

Total Index Entries: 129

About the Author

Timothy Ludwig is an author, historian, and publisher with over 25 years of creative and publishing experience. As the founder and owner of Rare Book Publishing LLC, he combines professional expertise with a lifelong dedication to exploring and preserving America's historical legacy. His work is characterized by meticulous research, respect for historical accuracy, and a passion for connecting past events to their continuing influence on the present.

Ludwig has spent decades studying and collecting artifacts that bring history to life, including Revolutionary War–era newspapers and books, Civil War soldiers' letters and photographs, and early American coins. These materials reflect his enduring fascination with the people, ideas, and conflicts that shaped the nation, and they continue to inspire his work — though the research for this book draws from a broad range of historical documents, records, and scholarly sources beyond his personal collection.

His previous book, Real Encounters: A Chronicle of Leprechaun and Fairy Accounts from Ireland, established his reputation for blending careful documentation with engaging narrative. Known for his ability to make complex historical topics accessible to modern readers, Ludwig approaches each project with both scholarly discipline and a storyteller's instinct.

In The Second Amendment: A History of the Right to Keep and Bear Arms in America, Ludwig traces the evolution of one of America's most debated constitutional principles from its colonial roots to the modern era. Through extensive historical research and thoughtful interpretation, he examines how the right to bear arms emerged, how it has been understood over time, and how it continues to shape conversations about liberty and individual rights today.

RareBookPublishing.com

www.ingramcontent.com/pod-product-compliance
Lightning Source LLC
LaVergne TN
LVHW051600080426
835510LV00020B/3068